iCare™

FACILITATOR MANUAL

FOR CHRISTIAN GRIEF SUPPORT GROUPS

EVERYTHING YOU NEED TO PLAN, PREPARE FOR & LEAD A CHRISTIAN GRIEF SUPPORT GROUP

INTERNATIONAL GRIEF INSTITUTE, LLC
COPYRIGHT © 2024

iCare Facilitator Manual for Christian Grief Support Groups– 2nd ed.
International Grief Institute, LLC
www.InternationalGriefInstitute.com

Cover Design by AlyBlue Media, LLC
Interior Design by AlyBlue Media LLC
Published by AlyBlue Media, LLC

ISBN: 978-1-950712-56-4
AlyBlue Media, LLC
Darby, Montana 59829 USA
www.AlyBlueMedia.com

PRINTED IN THE UNITED STATES OF AMERICA

CONTENTS

PREFACE

**The Bible is for healing,
sustenance and guidance.**

BY REV. ROLAND H. JOHNSON III

Griefwork—learning to live with a loved one in our heart instead of our arms—is a process of reconciliation, and the hardest work we'll ever do. It can strip our soul bare and leave us struggling for hope. The iCare program is carefully and thoughtfully designed to lead you through a compassionate 8-week program that will fuel you with comfort, understanding and hope by pairing Bible scriptures, self-care strategies, Bible journaling, and group time with others who speak a loss language.

The program offers useful and relevant tools that will support you as you begin to reconcile your head with your heart. Based upon balance, the program provides nourishment for your spiritual, physical and emotional selves along with strategies to help strengthen your natural, God-given resilience. Tending to your own needs now will serve you years down the road. As you regain your strength, you'll learn to become the light of hope for those behind you.

Group participants will learn:
- ☑ The value of sharing their emotions
- ☑ The role of self-care along the journey
- ☑ Powerful evidence-based healing modalities to strengthen their coping skills
- ☑ The role of resilience
- ☑ The comfort of Bible journaling
- ☑ That hope after loss is possible for everyone

Though the physical absence of our loved ones will always be keenly felt, loss and grief are a classroom through which we learn life's most valuable lessons. Love, support, God's word, and nurturing of our emotional, physical and spiritual selves can make all the difference between surviving and thriving. That's what the iCare program is all about.

LYNDA CHELDELIN FELL
International Grief Institute

Our Father who art in heaven,
hallowed be thy name.
Thy kingdom come.
Thy will be done
on earth as it is in heaven.
Give us this day our daily bread,
and forgive us our trespasses,
as we forgive those who trespass against us,
and lead us not into temptation,
but deliver us from evil.
For thine is the kingdom and the power, and the glory,
forever and ever.

In Jesus' name I pray, Amen.

iCare

CHAPTER 1
INTRODUCTION

Grieving doesn't stop when funeral services end.

SHERRY DEE MOBLEY

HOW TO USE THIS MANUAL

RECOMMENDATION

IGI recommends that regardless of loss type, grief support group facilitators should be a minimum of three years post loss, lest they risk needing more support than the participants.

Starting a Christian grief support group isn't hard, and can be a very rewarding experience. The iCare program is designed to provide participants with comfort and gentle guidance from a Christian facilitator with applied experience.

Whether you start a grief support group for one type of loss, or an open grief support group for all loss types, this eight-session program is carefully and thoughtfully designed to include the following key components:

- ✓ Discussion topics
- ✓ Helpful handouts
- ✓ Bible assignments
- ✓ Caring plan and self-care tips
- ✓ Bible journaling
- ✓ Personal connections

This manual includes everything you need to run a support group including instructions, forms, handouts, Bible scriptures and journaling, articles, Resilience Rx™ self-care tips, and more. All the handouts can be downloaded and printed from www.icarelibary.com/supportgroup. It also includes turnkey resources you or your organization can purchase as gifts for your grieving members, if desired.

The support group format is designed to run as an 8-session program but can be easily adapted to either a shorter or longer format if needed. It can also be adapted for a monthly drop-in group. At the conclusion, each participant will have had an opportunity to share and discuss common grief challenges, explore one another's journeys through faith, compile a self-care plan, engage in Bible exploring and journaling, and form lasting relationships and a network of support as they continue their individual journeys. Each workbook also includes useful articles for participants to explore in their own time.

IMPORTANCE OF SUPPORT GROUPS

Grief impacts and disrupts many areas of our lives. Without caring support, grief can impair a person's ability to move forward.

A good support group is multifaceted. The iCare format is designed to:

☑ Offer a supportive environment for people to externalize their emotions, verbalize Christian struggles in relation to loss, and talk about their deceased loved one.

☑ Introduce people to others who are going through a similar experience. This helps to normalize the grief experience.

☑ Offer opportunities to learn new ways of coping with situations by listening to the experiences of other participants.

☑ Offer a chance to chat, laugh, and learn that the heart can hold joy and sorrow at the same time.

☑ Provide relevant experiences to common challenges.

☑ Encourage Bible reading and journaling.

☑ Encourage self-care.

> **IMPORTANT**
>
> While a grief support group can be very therapeutic, it is not a therapy group nor a substitute for professional therapy.

Studies show that peer support is more effective than psychotherapy and has become the standard of care (International Critical Incident Stress Foundation, 2016).

Although peer support is only one stop on the overall continuum of care, group facilitators are a key component to the success of their participants. Because a solid understanding of grief is imperative to being able to guide others on their own journey, the first chapters in this manual include important information every grief group facilitator should know. These chapters include the fundamentals of the grief process including types, reactions and triggers, as well as important information about compassion fatigue.

BIBLE ASSIGNMENTS

Each of the eight sessions includes a Bible assignment that encourages participants to explore the Bible in their own time and find scriptures that comfort them. The Bible assignments also provide room for participants to journal feelings and emotions, and even write a letter to God. Journaling is a powerful evidence-based healing modality that should be encouraged.

WHAT DOES THE BIBLE SAY?

The iCare program offers scriptures as a talking point, but these are a starting point only. The Bible offers far more instruction and comfort than can be covered here. Encourage participants to read scripture slowly from a translation they understand, and to explore beyond the suggested scriptures. Much wisdom and insight are gained through reading the Bible, meditating upon its words and praying to God for understanding. The wisdom the Bible contains will help us walk the mourning journey as we continue to live and grow in faith.

Encourage participants to think about what they read and then reflect on the various levels of meaning and application through prayer. Remember, prayer is a conversation with God. It need not be formal. Invite participants to express how they feel to God. Even negative, confused or angry feelings are okay when you talk with the Lord.

REMEMBER ALWAYS . . .

Through Christ, we are a child of God. We are granted the privilege of God's personal attention and care through both good times and bad.

In **2 Samuel 18** tells the story of the death of Absalom, a favored son of King David. Though Absalom turned on his father, King David did all in his power to protect his son from harm. The scriptures carry the deep grief and emotion of King David at losing a son. The Book of Psalms, attributed to David, shares many deep emotions, feelings and great wisdom about the process of grief and one's relationship to God.

The story of Jacob's loss of his favorite son, Joseph, told in **Genesis 37**, reveals the struggle with inconsolable grief. The story of the coming Christ, from **Isaiah 53**, tells of the purpose of God's Son, Jesus Christ, bearing our grief and transgressions on our behalf. The New Testament proclaims hope, promise, relief and salvation from the grief, pain and suffering that fills our life. The resurrection of Christ and the promise of eternal life with God is the ultimate statement of hope for all who have experienced death of a loved one.

1 Peter 2 reminds us vividly that as believers in Christ we compose a royal priesthood, priest to each other, guaranteed the promise of eternal life and bound to help one another through all of life's trials and suffering. As a facilitator, you are fulfilling this role and encouraging others to do the same.

Bless your heart for serving as a light of hope for others.

NOTES:

CHAPTER 2
GRIEF 101

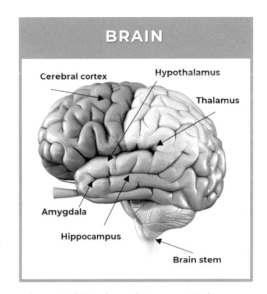

Grief is unique as one's fingerprint.

LYNDA CHELDELIN FELL

Grief is a normal reaction to loss and yet its complexity impacts the physiological, sociological, psychological, and spiritual self. It's important to note the following:

- All trauma has a grief associated with it, but not all grief has a trauma associated with it.

- Less complex losses, such as loss of a job, result in less complex grief. Profound, traumatic losses such as the unexpected death of a first-degree loved one, creates a psychological crisis with long-lasting effects on one's ability to cope and function.

- Grief's biological response is predictable but our emotional response—based upon our own inner resilience, adverse childhood experiences, personality type, access to social support, and more—is unique to each of us.

BIOLOGICAL RESPONSES

When emotional trauma occurs, it floods the brain with stress hormones, a response known as fight-or-flight syndrome. In response, parts of the brain are anesthetized. This causes time warp, tunnel vision, and memory loss and we tend to recall trauma events like a strobe light rather than a story. Biologically, the brain responds in a predictable pattern:

- **Brain stem** (the physical brain): Following a crisis, the brain stem is activated and the sympathetic nervous system sends the body into the fight, flight, freeze or fawn response. This involves over 120 different brain chemicals.

- **Limbic system** (the emotional brain): Second, the hippocampus, amygdala, and thalamus are stimulated. These structures regulate emotions, the storage of memories, and the interpretation of input from the senses. We remember the feelings associated with an event much more vividly than the details.

- **Cerebral cortex** (the thinking brain): The cerebral cortex is the least active part of the brain during a crisis. Complex thinking such as problem solving and decision-making are somewhat impaired, and explains why people become confused and have difficulty with options.

COGNITIVE AFFECTS

Psychologically, every event is interpreted through a number of filters unique to each person including:

- Physical proximity to the event
- Relational proximity to the event
- History of prior trauma
- Support system
- Personality

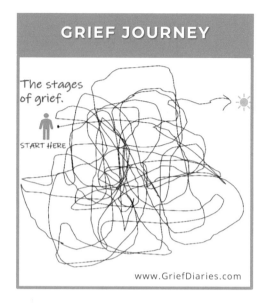

GRIEF JOURNEY

The stages of grief.

START HERE

www.GriefDiaries.com

Cognitively, grief is a highly distracting process that diverts our emotional bandwidth and creates fears both rational and irrational. During the acute stage of grief, people are actively processing what happened. Healing begins in subsequent stages rather than right away.

Not all people respond the same way to death of a loved one. The emotional impact depends on a number of factors including inner resilience, personality, childhood experiences, and availability of support through family, friends, and coworkers. Some have more severe, longer-lasting reactions.

Lack of sufficient support can overwhelm a person's ability to cope and result in distress, impairment and dysfunction. Influencing factors also include:

- the extent of exposure to the event
- the amount of support during the loss event and its aftermath
- the amount of personal loss and social disruption

Grief reactions

Though the nature and scope of grief differs, common reactions occur in 6 distinct categories.

- ☑ Cognitive
- ☑ Emotional
- ☑ Behavioral
- ☑ Physical
- ☑ Social
- ☑ spiritual

IMPORTANT

Any sign or symptom of abnormal reactions warrant referral to a higher level of care. **Refer whenever in doubt.**

Understanding what are normal reactions is necessary to understand how to provide support.

COGNITIVE REACTIONS

NORMAL REACTIONS

- Forgetfulness
- Poor concentration
- Low productivity
- Negative Attitude
- Confusion
- Guilt
- Preoccupation with loss event

ABNORMAL REACTIONS

- Suicidal/homicidal ideation
- Paranoid ideation
- Dissociation
- Disabling guilt
- Hallucinations
- Delusions
- Persistent helplessness

BEHAVIORAL REACTIONS

NORMAL REACTIONS

- 1000-yard stare
- Hyperstartle
- Sleep disturbance
- Crying spells
- Isolation
- Resentment
- Increased risk-taking
- Distrust
- Withdrawal
- Impulsiveness

ABNORMAL REACTIONS

- Violence
- Antisocial acts
- Abuse of others
- Long-tem diminished personal hygiene
- Self harm
- Immobility
- Self medication

EMOTIONAL REACTIONS

NORMAL REACTIONS

- Anxiety
- Frustration and/or irritability
- Mood swings
- Temper outbursts
- Nightmares
- Crying spells

ABNORMAL REACTIONS

- Panic attacks
- Immobilizing depression
- PTSD
- Impaired functioning
- Infantile emotions

PHYSICAL REACTIONS

NORMAL REACTIONS	ABNORMAL REACTIONS
▪ Change in appetite	▪ Chest pain
▪ Headaches	▪ Irregular heartbeats
▪ Fatigue	▪ Recurrent dizziness
▪ Insomnia	▪ Recurrent headaches
▪ Weight change	▪ Collapse/loss of consciousness
▪ Restlessness	▪ Numbness
▪ Upset stomach	

RED FLAGS

All evidence of physical dysfunction should be taken seriously and referred to a physician, even if it seems ambiguous.

Any complaint of chest pain and/or difficulty breathing warrants immediate medical attention, even if you suspect nothing more than heartburn. Unless you're a trained medical professional, don't try to diagnose the symptoms. **Immediately call 911 and let medics triage the person and determine next steps.**

SPIRITUAL REACTIONS

NORMAL REACTIONS	ABNORMAL REACTIONS
▪ Emptiness	▪ Religious hallucinations
▪ Loss of meaning	▪ Religious delusions
▪ Doubt	
▪ Unforgiving	
▪ Loss of direction	
▪ Cynicism	
▪ Extreme or sudden religiosity	
▪ Cessation from practice of faith	

iCare

SOCIAL REACTIONS

NORMAL REACTIONS	ABNORMAL REACTIONS
▪ Family strife ▪ Altered friendships ▪ Changes in workplace ▪ Altered social status ▪ Role redefinitions ▪ Loss of motivation ▪ Loss of perspective ▪ Goal reorientation	▪ Longterm withdrawal from all social contacts ▪ Quitting employment ▪ Total reassociation with antisocial groups ▪ Running away, disappearing

RED FLAGS

Beyond intense physical complaints, there are **3 reactions** that are never normal and are red flags for immediate evaluation:

- Suicidal thoughts with plan and intent
- Homicidal thoughts with plan and intent
- Hallucinations and/or delusions

It isn't uncommon for vague and fleeting suicidal thoughts to occur following death of a close loved one, but a formal mental health evaluation will help determine the danger level. **If unsure, call 911 and let them guide you.**

Grief types

Just as the grief journey is unique to each of us, there are also numerous types of grief. Below are the most common types you're likely to encounter in support group participants.

NORMAL GRIEF

A normal reaction to a loss event.

ANTICIPATORY GRIEF

Grieving an anticipated death before it occurs, common when a loved one is dying from a terminal illness.

TRAUMATIC GRIEF

Experiencing a sudden and unexpected loss; common when one has witnessed the actual death event.

CUMULATIVE GRIEF

Experiencing a second loss while still grieving a prior loss. Also known as **grief overload**.

COMPLICATED GRIEF

An ongoing, heightened state of mourning that is debilitating, and incapacitates on a long-term basis. It's a grief reaction that occurs when one fails to work through their loss, continually experiencing extreme distress with no progress towards feeling better and no improvement in day-to-day functioning.

DELAYED GRIEF

Reacting much later to a death than is typical due to initial avoidance of the loss and emotional pain.

MASKED GRIEF

A reaction that impairs normal functioning without the individual recognizing that the behaviors are related to the loss. Symptoms are often masked as either physical symptoms or other maladaptive behaviors.

DISENFRANCHISED GRIEF

A rejection of one's mourning by their culture, family, social or work environment. The grief and suffering are disqualified by those around the mourner.

ABSENT GRIEF

Reacting to a major loss by blocking one's feelings as though it never happened. The individual shows no reaction at all and fails to give it importance in his or her life.

Grief triggers

Grief triggers are anything that brings up memories related to the loss and spark anxiety and/or emotional outbursts. Little reminders that throw us back in time and ambush emotions, they can happen anytime, anywhere, and be severe enough to induce a panic attack.

If someone is struggling with severe triggers and panic attacks, encourage them to seek the care of their primary medical provider.

> ## WHAT TO KNOW
>
> Triggers are a normal and common component of the grief process and should never be minimized, even if you don't understand it.

TRIGGER EXAMPLES

- Spotting someone in the crowd who looks like our deceased loved one.
- The first flush of our deceased loved one's favorite flower.
- Scene of an accident.
- Sight of a hospital or favorite restaurant chain.
- Scent of loved one's cologne, perfume, flowers, food, etc.
- Sound of a song, train whistle, baby crying, horn honking, certain TV commercial, etc.
- A certain moment in time such as 11:30 p.m. when the original call came notifying the family of their loved one's death
- Holidays, birthdays, anniversaries.

WHAT TO KNOW

- People experiencing the same loss may not have the same triggers.
- Triggers may or may not lessen with time.
- Triggers can be subtle or surprising.

HOW YOU CAN HELP

- Reassure them they're safe.
- Remind them to breathe.
- Avoid minimizing the trigger's significance even if you don't understand it.
- Hold the space for the mourner to work through it on their own.

Ripple effect

Death has a ripple effect in that the death of the loved one is a primary loss that often results in secondary losses. While the initial death event is public, many secondary losses are less obvious and often go unobserved by outsiders. Some of the secondary losses include:

- ◆ Loss of family structure
    - o A widow who now lives alone and has to manage all the household responsibilities.
    - o A child who lost a parent and now lives in a single parent household.
    - o A child who lost a sibling also lost a playmate.

- ◆ Loss of identity
    - o When an only child dies, is the mother still a mother? Is the father still a father?
    - o When a spouse dies, the widow/widower must adjust from being half of a pair to being alone.

- ◆ Loss of lifestyle
    - o A parent who volunteered for the child's school or sports team, and now does so no longer.
    - o A widow who has to adjust to being single again, and often is forced to find support outside his/her married friends.

Many mourners also experience a loss of self after death of a loved one. Understanding grief and these secondary losses is important to understanding your families and their reactions to grief.

CHAPTER 3
SUICIDAL & HOMICIDAL IDEATION

No matter what happens, or how bad it seems today, life does go on and it will be better tomorrow.

MAYA ANGELOU

Suicidal ideation is the thought process of having ideas or ruminating about the possibility of taking one's own life. It is not a diagnosis yet is a symptom that isn't uncommon during intense grief. You might hear statements similar to the following:

"I feel so sad, and just want the pain to stop."

"I don't think I can live without my loved one. How can I possibly go on?"

"I pray every night that I won't wake up in the morning. I have nothing to live for."

Homicidal ideation is the thought process of having ideas or ruminating about the possibility of taking the lives of others.

What do you do or say? How do you know whether this is the grief talking, whether the participant has slid into a depression that warrants medical care, or whether your participant is really going to act?

The simple fact is that you don't know, but through questions, you can triage the participant to gauge how likely s/he is to act on it.

STATEMENTS TO AVOID:

Statements that minimize the participant's emotions can be unhelpful, and possibly more damaging. Statements to avoid include the following:

- "Surely you don't mean that."
- "Think about your family. How could you do that to them?"
- "You have so much to live for."

The goal at this moment is to encourage the participant to verbalize his/her feelings. Doing so will also help you triage the danger level for how serious this is so you have as much information as possible when you notify emergency resources.

WHAT TO KNOW:

Thoughts about suicide or homicide may be as detailed as a formulated plan without the suicidal or homicidal act itself. The range of suicidal or homicidal ideation varies greatly from detailed planning, role playing, self-harm and actual attempts, which may be deliberately constructed to be discovered, or where death may be fully intended.

WHAT TO KNOW

Suicide happens when pain level exceeds coping skills.

Sometimes threats are vague or ambiguous, and/or may be aimed at a future event or time. These threats should be taken seriously.

WHAT DOES THE BIBLE SAY?

The topic of suicide is a difficult discussion in Christian faith, and often triggers strong reactions and judgment. Should the topic of suicidal ideation arise during group time, remind participants that God knows a person's heart and it is up to God to handle such judgments.

Whether a participant is having suicidal ideation and/or lost a loved one to suicide, it's important to support that individual rather than condemning his/her emotions and/or the actions of their loved one. Condemnation in a support group is a form of public shaming that serves no purpose in God's eyes. As a Christian, we want to serve as a light of hope until a person is strong enough to hold their own light once again. Leave the judgment up to God.

The Bible itself can be comforting for those who are struggling with suicidal or homicidal ideation. Also, **James 5:16** tells us to pray for one another, that the effective, fervent prayer of a righteous man avails much. Both individual prayer and intercessory prayer are ways we can bring the needs of others before God through Christ. Should a participant reveal suicidal ideation during group time, consider stopping the session to lead the group in intercessory prayer on behalf of that participant. Anyone in the group can lead intercessory prayer. It need not take long, and can be a powerful experience for all who witness and participate. Be sure to ask permission of the suffering participant first. If s/he declines, invite participants to pray for that person individually from home.

MORE STRATEGIES:

- Acknowledge the validity of the participant's feelings and ask fact-gathering questions. One approach might be to say, "How long have you been struggling with this thought?"

- Avoid telling the participant that suicide is a sin, and don't allow other participants to have their say on this subject. If necessary, remind participants that we're there to support one another, not condemn. Regardless of one's belief, such a statement implies condemnation instead of support. Such condemnation is likely to shut him/her down and possibly provoke deepening suicidal ideation because he/she feels a failure in God's eyes.

- Address the group to see if others have felt this way either now or in the past. This can help the suicidal participant feel validated in his/her emotions, and less alone.

- Triage the severity of the situation by asking the participant the following questions. The answers can be important to pass along to emergency personnel.

  ❏ Is there a definite plan for dying by suicide or acting on the homicidal impulse, such as time, place and/or method?

  ❏ How intense are the impulses?

  ❏ How long has the person had suicidal or homicidal ideation?

  ❏ Are others involved in the plan? If so, how?

  ❏ Was there a precipitating event? Why is suicide or homicide being considered now?

  ❏ Is there a history of suicidality or homicidal ideation in the past, or in the family?

- **Promote hope** by listening to the participant. Invite him/her to talk about the reasons why s/he wants to die and try not to interrupt so they can verbalize their emotions around this. Your listening skills can help determine the severity of the situation.

- **Share referrals.** Have your resources on hand. While arranging for help, stay with the participant. Do not leave him/her alone.

- **Inform the participant that when they are a danger to themselves or others, you cannot maintain professional confidentiality.**

> **RESOURCES**
>
> **Emergency:** 911
>
> **National Suicide Prevention Lifeline:** 1-800-273-TALK (8255)
>
> **Crisis Text Line:** text TALK to 741741

YOUR ROLE

Unless you are professionally trained and certified to handle suicide or homicidal interventions, do not under any circumstances attempt an intervention. Your role is to:

- Acknowledge and validate the suicidal or homicidal feelings
- Triage the situation by eliciting information
- Pass this information along to emergency personnel

TRIAGING GUIDELINES

Ask the following questions in order to gain a better understanding of the scope of imminent danger. Your triage of the situation can be immensely helpful when passing this information along to emergency services and/or law enforcement authorities.

  ❏ Does the participant want to attempt suicide or homicide?

  ❏ Does the participant have a plan to attempt suicide or homicide?

  ❏ Does the participant have the means to carry out that plan?

  ❏ Has the participant ever attempted suicide or homicide in the past?

  ❏ If so, what methods of attempt have been used in the past?

The answers to these questions will help emergency services determine the depth of the situation. If the participant has a plan and access to a lethal means, is planning to make an attempt very soon, or is currently in the process of making an attempt, this person is in imminent danger and should not be left alone. Call 911 immediately.

RED FLAGS !

If you do not have the training or knowledge to conduct a suicide risk assessment and determine the safety of a participant, call 911. When a person's life is in danger, safety takes priority over privacy.

CHAPTER 4
COMPASSION FATIGUE

A disorder that affects those who do their work well.

DR. CHARLES FIGLEY

Managing the wellbeing of a support group starts with managing the wellbeing of its facilitator. This must be every facilitator's first priority. As a grief support group facilitator, it's important to guard against compassion fatigue especially when practicing emotional regulation.

Also known as **vicarious traumatization** or **secondary traumatic stress**, compassion fatigue is a cumulative physical, emotional and psychological effect of listening to traumatic stories or events that aren't your own. It is emotional burnout attributed to the cost of caring for others and occurs when we help others without recharging our own batteries.

THE COST OF CARING

Anyone who cares for others is someone who has a higher risk of suffering from compassion fatigue. By the numbers (Gaille, 2017):

♦ 87% of emergency responders have reported symptoms of compassion fatigue.

♦ 70% of mental health professionals have experienced compassion fatigue.

♦ 1 in 2 child welfare workers experience symptoms of compassion fatigue in the severe range.

KEYNOTE

♦ Vicarious trauma is the cumulative effect of working with survivors.

♦ It is characterized by deep emotional and physical exhaustion.

♦ Symptoms resemble depression and PTSD.

♦ It can strike the most caring professionals.

SYMPTOMS

Symptoms of compassion fatigue can be subtle or stark. Below are the most common signs to look for.

- Emotional exhaustion & irritability
- Physical exhaustion
- Mental exhaustion
- Difficulty concentrating & clinical errors
- Lapse in judgment with client boundaries
- Reduced sense of meaning in work
- Struggle to complete assignments and tasks
- Dreading work

MOTHER TERESA

Mother Teresa mandated her nuns take an entire year off from their duties every 4-5 years to allow them to heal from the effects of their caregiving work (Stress.org).

Compassion fatigue vs burnout

Compassion fatigue and burnout share many of the same symptoms. So, what's the difference?

- ✓ Compassion fatigue has a more rapid onset.
- ✓ Burnout is a slow burn that emerges over time.
- ✓ When managed early, compassion fatigue has a faster recovery.

The cost

How compassion fatigue affects us at work:

- ✓ Absenteeism
- ✓ Presenteeism
- ✓ Decreased productivity
- ✓ Clinical errors
- ✓ Lapse in judgment
- ✓ High turnover rate
- ✓ Cost to Corporate America: $48 billion per year (Gaille, 2017)

If you feel an emotional burnout, it's important to share this with someone you trust. The longer you let it go, the harder it can be to recover from.

Resilience

Human resilience is the ability to resist, recover from, or adapt to difficulties. When faced with a challenge, there are three possible outcomes:

1. Full recovery and ability to function
2. Partial recovery and stunted ability to function
3. No recovery and halted function (burnout)

Stress management and human resilience are complementary. Building and strengthening resilience through strategies that support the brain, body, and emotions can help mitigate stress, and prevent compassion fatigue and burnout.

Management

Because compassion fatigue occurs when we help others without recharging our own batteries, proactively managing stress before it gets out of control builds positive buffering habits that can ultimately help to avoid prolonged stress and compassion fatigue.

You can't pour from an empty cup. If you feel the symptoms of compassion fatigue or emotional burnout, it's important to share this. The longer you let it go, the harder it can be to recover from. Below are management tips to help mitigate compassion fatigue symptoms before they lead to burnout.

EASY MANAGEMENT HOW-TO

- ✓ Understand how stress affects you by completing the ABCDs of prevention on the next page

- ✓ Understand how resilience can offset stress and compassion fatigue

- ✓ Engage in activities that trigger the brain to secrete positive hormones

- ✓ Set emotional boundaries

- ✓ Maintain a healthy work-life balance

- ✓ Stay hydrated

- ✓ Eat for health

- ✓ Strive for restorative sleep

> **KEYNOTE**
>
> Proactively developing and regularly practicing positive stress-buffering habits can offset stress.

YOU CAN'T POUR FROM AN Empty Cup. TAKE CARE OF YOURSELF FIRST.

The ABCDs of prevention

Evaluate your personal ABCDs of self care by answering the questions below. Then create a toolbox of things you enjoy to offset the stress in your life using the Resilience Rx evidence-based modalities in this manual.

A = AWARENESS

❑ What type of stories do you take home with you?

❑ What external stressors are going on in your life?

B = BALANCE

❑ How do you set emotional boundaries? How often do you set these boundaries?

❑ What restores and replenishes you?

C = CONNECTIONS

❑ How strong is your support system?

❑ What connections do you have to like-minded activity groups?

D = DECONTAMINATION

❑ What mindful strategies or rituals do you use to decontaminate your mind from stories that bother you?

CHAPTER 5
HOW TO FACILITATE A SUPPORT GROUP

You are there to empathize and facilitate.

VIV ALBERTINE

Facilitating and co-facilitating a Christian support group is a very rewarding experience. When you facilitate a support group, you're giving your time to help others. When we help others, it pleases God and helps our own hearts to heal.

VALUE OF A SUPPORT GROUP

Grief support groups offer participants the comfort and comradery that comes from a shared experience. Support groups discourage isolation and offer empathetic understanding from others who can relate. It also provides an opportunity for social interaction in a safe, nurturing environment.

A well-run support group offers a nonjudgmental atmosphere where participants feel safe and secure enough to share their feelings and struggles. A grief support group can be ongoing, or they can have a predetermined number of sessions with a start and stop date, as determined by the facilitator's commitment.

Facilitating a support group comes with responsibilities for planning, preparing, and leading. This chapter outlines those responsibilities along with tips to set you up for success.

The iCare program is topic-focused and designed for 8 group sessions. Discussions are focused on the challenges commonly encountered along the grief journey, providing an opportunity for participants to externalize their own struggles. Questions related to the topic are posed to the group and participants are invited to share their personal experiences in relation to that topic.

Each session includes the following:

- ✓ Emotional check-in
- ✓ Bible work check-in
- ✓ One to two discussion topics
- ✓ Helpful handouts
- ✓ Caring plan tip
- ✓ Bible reading and journaling

TOPICS

The topics cover challenges that most people experience along their own grief journey. Although not every topic will be applicable to everyone, most will learn something from that session's topic, even if it doesn't apply to them.

HANDOUTS

Session handouts are included in the workbooks. If a participant shows up without a workbook, you may print the handouts from www.icarelibrary.com/supportgroup or copy the handouts from this manual to tide them over until they have their own workbook. Workbooks are available from any bookseller including Amazon as well as www.InternationalGriefInstitute.com. Unless otherwise indicated, most handouts are designed to be read at home, not during the session.

CARING PLAN

Self-care is always important, and is especially so during the grief journey. We can't always predict loss and other stressors, but practicing self-help techniques that tend to our physical, mental, emotional, and spiritual needs can help us cope. Bottom line is true for everyone: **when we feel better, we cope better.**

> ### WHAT TO KNOW
> Bible work and caring plans are designed to be done at home.

At the end of each session is an opportunity for **Bible work** and a **Resilience Rx™** tip to consider adding to their self-care plan. The goal is to offer self-help strategies that trigger positive hormones—dopamine, serotonin, and oxytocin—to help support both you and your participants as they learn to move forward with their loved one in their heart instead of their arms. Encourage participants to try each Resilience Rx™ strategy at least once.

FACILITATOR RESPONSIBILITIES

A support group facilitator's role is to stimulate discussions that are designed to support and encourage progress toward reconciliation for each participant. A facilitator's main function is to foster communication among the group and to model effective interaction that participants can emulate. Facilitators also provide an example of how to share in the group.

> ### IMPORTANT
> Monitor yourself from getting too close and wanting to fix people (interfering with resiliency). It's also important to know when you're over your head.

One of the values of a support group is that participants have a chance to verbalize their emotions in a nurturing, safe environment. Because a support group is an important healing modality after loss, it's critical that facilitators ensure that every participant feels welcome and safe. This means that facilitators must enforce confidentiality and group boundaries for everyone's benefit.

HELPFUL TIPS:

✓ Ensure each participant completes a registration prior to the first session. The registration is a one-time form that provides participant contact information. Keep these on hand for your own records. Use the registration form on page 31.

✓ Bring a small spiral notebook to keep notes when needed, though avoid appearing as though you're documenting the entire evening. You don't need to keep detailed notes, just things you don't want to forget or action items you need to do between sessions. Use the **My Participants** sheet on page 33 to keep pertinent details about your participants so you can avoid saying, "Now, who did you lose again?"

✓ Place chairs in a circle if possible, with an open space in the middle. Circle seating avoids a hierarchy of authority and conveys the tone that participants and facilitators are equal. A circle also allows the entire group to be visible to one another without having to look behind oneself to see who is talking. Manage the group by keeping the discussion moving around the circle.

✓ Using the sign-in sheet on page 32, ensure that every participant signs in at the beginning of every session. This helps you to recall who was present at any given meeting, should you need to. We recommend you keep both the registration and sign-in forms for at least three years.

✓ Mic and audio/visual equipment generally aren't needed.

✓ Refreshments aren't required but nice to have on hand. Most support groups have bottled water, coffee, tea, and a snack available. To avoid buying refreshments out of your own pocket, ask a local store, café or bakery to donate. Consider rotating which stores you solicit from so as not to depend on one store.

✓ Speak using simple words. Avoid using professional or academic verbiage so everyone understands what is said.

✓ Practice good listening skills and maintain supportive neutrality. Don't criticize anyone for what they've said, even if you don't agree. It's important to not invalidate their experience.

✓ Some participants will participate more than others. Meet each one where they are without expectation, though encourage participation and make sure everyone has a chance to share.

✓ Monitor the group for emotional and physical red flags, and handle appropriately.

✓ The participant who is talking should be the center of attention. Side conversations can be disruptive, and make the sharer feel invalidated. Don't allow that.

✓ Keep on hand local community resources to offer participants when needed. You can place these on a side table for participants to take as needed. Be sure to keep it up to date.

SNAPSHOT OF THE FIRST MEETING

1. Make sure you have a completed registration on hand for each participant.

2. Make sure each participant signs in at the beginning of each session so you have record of who was and wasn't there. Don't rely on your own memory.

3. Use nametags if needed to help participants get to know one another. Be sure to wear your own nametag for the first couple sessions.

4. Start the meeting on time by welcoming everyone.

5. Introduce yourself and then, using the circle format, invite each participant to introduce themselves by asking them to share the following:

   a. Their first name

   b. The first name of their deceased loved one and their relationship (child, spouse, etc)

   c. The age their loved one was and the year s/he died

   d. The cause of death

6. Review the ground rules for the group meetings.

7. Begin the session with an emotional check-in, then a Bible work check-in, then introducing that night's topic for discussion. If a participant poses a question related to that topic, allow each participant to weigh in.

8. At the end of the meeting, thank the participants for being there and being proactive about managing their own grief.

9. Close the meeting with a prayer, poem or group hug.

> **IMPORTANT**
>
> Since being the facilitator can be viewed as a leadership position, some participants may become dependent on the facilitator. To reduce the potential for dependency, encourage and emphasize individual strengths.

ESTABLISH GROUND RULES

Ground rules are important to keep the support group running smoothly and keep it productive for everyone. Ensuring etiquette will help keep the discussion on track, minimize side conversations, and make it easier to mitigate disruptions. A good set of ground rules will avoid ambiguity, encourage participation, and help participants feel comfortable when sharing sensitive experiences.

BUT . . . GROUND RULES ARE ONLY EFFECTIVE WHEN THEY'RE FOLLOWED.

Ground rules are important to keep the group functioning. Review **Ground Rules** on page 43 with the group and reiterate the following:

- Raise your hand if you have something to say if it isn't your turn to talk.

- Listen to what other people are saying.

- No mocking, judging, or interrupting.

- Respect each other. No criticizing.

- No profanity or offensive language.

- Don't give advice. Avoid beginning any sentence with "You should . . . "

- Silence your cell phones to minimize disruption.

- Grief can make participants feel emotionally raw. Sometimes, this can lead to anger. Validate the anger by acknowledging it and offer a gentle reminder that no two grief journeys are alike—what might make one participant feel angry might actual comfort another.

EMOTIONAL REGULATION

Emotional regulation is the ability to exhibit sympathy, compassion and support while controlling one's own emotions in the face of the emotional distress of another. Good emotional regulation includes the ability to:

☑ Recognize your own emotional response and accept it rather than reject it

☑ Engage in impulse control when upset

☑ Engage in strategies to reduce the intensity of the emotion

By practicing the above techniques, facilitators will be better equipped to handle the challenges of being emotionally involved and impacted by the participants in the support group.

COMMUNITY RESOURCES

Use the list below to identify the resources in your community, and keep a list with current contact information on hand to give to participants.

- Other groups being held in the community

- Local bereavement organizations (if any)

- Hospice center

- Library resource center

- Senior center

- Crisis hotline number

- Funeral homes

SUGGESTED OPENING PRAYER:

Heavenly Father,

We come before you today in humility and faith.
We thank you for all the blessings in our lives.
We ask for your guidance and wisdom as we
minister to and share our losses with one another.
Please help us to keep an open heart and fill us
with courage, strength, patience and grace.

We ask these things in your name, Amen.

CHAPTER 6
READY, SET, GO!

Encourage, lift, and strengthen one another.
DEBORAH DAY

<table>
<tr><td colspan="2">**3 EASY STEPS**</td></tr>
<tr><td>1.</td><td>Plan out your group</td></tr>
<tr><td>2.</td><td>Prepare for your group</td></tr>
<tr><td>3.</td><td>Lead your group</td></tr>
</table>

Now that you have a solid understanding of grief, compassion fatigue, the responsibilities and ground rules of leading a support group, you're ready to plan, prepare, and lead. This chapter outlines how to do that.

PLAN

❑ **CO-FACILITATOR**. Decide who is going to be your co-facilitator. Although this is optional, the benefits of having a co-facilitator is to share responsibilities, avoid disruption if one facilitator falls ill, and having an extra person to minister to a participant who might leave the session in distress.

My co-facilitator will be: _____

❑ **MAX PARTICIPANTS**. Decide on the maximum number of participants you can accommodate. If you have the space and more than 15 registered participants, consider splitting into two groups, with one facilitator per group. If the space isn't large enough to accommodate all who register, consider dividing it into two different groups held on different days.

My max number of participants will be: _____

❑ **DATE/TIME.** Choose your dates and meeting time. Depending on the demographics of your participants, most support groups run in the evening to accommodate those who work traditional hours.

o Decide whether your sessions will run weekly or monthly
o Decide whether your sessions will run in the morning, afternoon, or evening

SESSION FREQUENCY: ☐ WEEKLY ☐ MONTHLY

START DATE: _____ **STOP DATE:** _____

START TIME: _____ **STOP TIME:** _____

❑ **FORMAT.** Choose whether you're going with an open format or a closed format.

  ○ If closed, participants can join only in the beginning and must register ahead of time. Decide how you're going to send out and collect registrations.

  ○ If open, can anyone from the community attend including family members and/or the media?

My format choice is: ☐ **OPEN** ☐ **CLOSED**

❑ **REGISTRATION.** If going with a closed group, create your registration process. Preregister participants using the registration form on page 31.

❑ **TYPE.** Choose whether you're going with general loss that will include a mix of loss types, or stick with one loss language, such as those who have lost a loved one to suicide. Will you allow both men and women? Will you require a minimum age?

The group type will be: ☐ **GENERAL LOSS** ☐ **SPECIFIC LOSS:** _____

The group will be: ☐ **WOMEN ONLY** ☐ **MEN ONLY** ☐ **BOTH**

The minimum age, if any, will be: _____

❑ **LENGTH.** Decide on your meeting length. Will you end abruptly after 90 minutes? Or will you allow 2 hours to accommodate socializing over refreshments after the meeting ends?

The session length will be: ☐ **90 minutes** ☐ **2 hours**

❑ **LOCATION.** If your church doesn't have space, secure meeting space that has ample, well lit parking that is easy to access, adequate bathroom facilities, and can accommodate your schedule. Consider the following options:

- Personal home
- Community library room
- Community conference room

- Hospital conference room
- Place of worship community room
- Funeral home community room

Meeting location: _____

Address: _____

Location contact: _____ **Phone:** _____

❑ **DIRECTIONS.** Prepare directions and email them to registrants or include in advertising.

❑ **SIGNAGE.** Determine location of sandwich board signage and place it prior to the start of each meeting so participants can easily find you.

☐ **REFRESHMENTS**. Decide on refreshments. Bottled water, coffee, tea, and a snack are common but not mandatory. Consider soliciting from local bakers or using a sign-up sheet to invite participants to take turns supplying refreshments.

☐ **WORKBOOKS**. Purchase workbooks, if desired. This will eliminate the need for you to print session handouts, and will give participants a tangible visual for their individual progress. Ask participants to reimburse you at the first session, if desired, but be sure they're aware before-hand of this expense.

☐ **ADVERTISING**. Notify local organizations of your newly formed support group so they can pass along the invitation. Consider notifying the following:

o Churches

o Hospice groups

o Hospitals and other healthcare agencies

o Counseling agencies

o Local colleges

o Local newspapers

o Local radio stations

o Local TV stations

PREPARE

Once you've planned out your support group, you can begin to prepare for success. Use the following checklist to help get things ready.

☐ **REGISTRATION.** Send out registrations (if going with a closed format). Be sure to include a due date and where to return completed registrations. Keep completed forms on file.

☐ **MY PARTICIPANTS**. If going with a closed format, prepare and complete My Participants form to help you remember key details about each participant. Take this with you to each session but keep it in a discrete place to avoid exposing potentially sensitive information.

☐ **SIGN-IN.** Prepare your sign-in sheet for each session and keep on file so you don't have to rely on memory who was present.

☐ **GROUND RULES.** Prepare and print the ground rules to distribute to participants at the first session. Keep a stack on hand at subsequent sessions.

☐ **HANDOUTS.** Prepare and print extra handouts to have on hand for those who show up with-out a workbook. Printable PDFs are available at icarelibrary.com/supportgroup.

☐ **NAMETAGS.** Prepare nametags or have blank ones on hand. Don't forget your own.

☐ **RESOURCES.** Prepare a typed list of local and online resources. Keep list current and up to date. Give to participants at first meeting. Have a stack available at subsequent meetings.

☐ **SUPPLIES.** Consider purchasing the following to have on hand at each session:

o Nametags

o Tissue

o Spiral notebook and pen for notes

o Refreshments, if desired

LEAD

The time has finally come to facilitate your first session. Once you have a few sessions under your belt, your confidence and facilitation skills will increase, making you an asset to your community. Use the checklist below to help you keep things running smoothly.

1. **ARRIVE**. Arrive 30 minutes prior to set up before participants arrive.

2. **ROOM**. Set up room for success.

   a. Arrange an adequate number of chairs in one circle.

   b. Utilize a side table for sign-in, registrations, handouts, and refreshments.

   c. Adjust the room temperature and lighting. Keep it sufficiently light but not bright.

3. **WELCOME**. Greet participants at the door.

   a. Have each participant fill out a registration form if they haven't already done so.

   b. Have each participant sign in on sign-in sheet.

   c. Ask participants to wear a nametag.

4. **BEGIN**.

   a. Facilitators sit at opposite ends of the circle.

   b. Start on time.

   c. Open with the prayer on page 26, if desired, then Introduce facilitators and share the facilitator's role (first session only).

   d. Emphasize that group support isn't counseling (each session).

   e. Share any housekeeping information, such as where the bathrooms and garbage cans are located (first session only).

   f. Review support group Ground Rules (first session only).

   g. See individual sessions in this manual for instructions for each session topic.

   h. End on time. Make this mandatory to honor participant schedules (and your own).

   i. Plan to stay 30 minutes after closing to clean up. It's okay to allow socializing among participants while you do this, but make sure you are the last to leave and the facility is locked behind you (if after hours).

   j. At the end of the final session, invite participants to complete and submit an anonymous evaluation.

SUPPORT GROUP PARTICIPANT REGISTRATION

NAME		PHONE:	
ADDRESS:		EMERGENCY CONTACT & PHONE:	
CITY:		YOUR AGE:	

PLEASE DESCRIBE YOUR LOSS:

NAME OF DECEASED:	
RELATIONSHIP TO YOU:	
DATE OF DEATH:	
AGE AT TIME OF DEATH:	
CAUSE OF DEATH:	

Name and relationship of others currently living in your home:

What else would you like the facilitator(s) to know about you?

SUPPORT GROUP SIGN-IN SHEET

GROUP NAME		MEETING DATE:	
FACILITATOR 1:		PHONE:	
FACILITATOR 2:		PHONE:	
PARTICIPANT NAME:		PARTICIPANT PHONE:	

F02/SUPPORT GROUP SIGN-IN

MY PARTICIPANTS

PARTICIPANT NAME:	LOSS TYPE	LOVED ONE'S NAME	YEAR OF LOSS
EXAMPLE: Judy Smith	Husband	Harold	2019

SUPPORT GROUP EVALUATION

PLEASE HELP US EVALUATE OUR SUPPORT GROUP	
YOUR NAME (optional):	
YOUR LOSS:	
DATE OF LOSS:	

FACILITATOR RATING

Did the facilitator(s) create a welcoming and supportive environment?   ❐ Yes   ❐ No

COMMENTS:

Were the facilitator(s) effective at keeping each session flowing?   ❐ Yes   ❐ No

COMMENTS:

Were the facilitator(s) effective at communicating?   ❐ Yes   ❐ No

COMMENTS:

Were the facilitator(s) effective at listening?   ❐ Yes   ❐ No

COMMENTS:

GROUP RATING

Do you feel the session topics were helpful?   ❐ Yes   ❐ No

COMMENTS:

Do you feel the Bible work was useful?   ❐ Yes   ❐ No

COMMENTS:

Do you feel the resilience exercises were helpful?   ❐ Yes   ❐ No

COMMENTS:

Do you feel the support group met your needs?   ❐ Yes   ❐ No

COMMENTS:

How would you rate this group?   ❐ Poor   ❐ Fair   ❐ Good   ❐ Very good   ❐ Excellent

COMMENTS:

What suggestions do you have to improve this support group?

COMMENTS:

LIST OF HANDOUTS & ASSIGNMENTS

SESSION 1: LOSS & GRIEF

- ❑ HANDOUT 01:   Ground rules
- ❑ HANDOUT 02:   Reacting to loss
- ❑ HANDOUT 03:   Grief stages
- ❑ HANDOUT 04:   A word about resilience
- ❑ HANDOUT 05:   RESILIENCE RX: Create your care plan
- ❑ HANDOUT 06:   Benefits of journaling
- ❑ HANDOUT 07:   Bible work

SESSION 2: COPING WITH TRIGGERS

- ❑ HANDOUT 08:   Coping with triggers
- ❑ HANDOUT 09:   Ripple effect
- ❑ HANDOUT 10:   Societal myths about loss
- ❑ HANDOUT 11:   RESILIENCE RX: Sensory therapy
- ❑ HANDOUT 12:   Bible work

SESSION 3: GRIEF STRESS

- ❑ HANDOUT 13:   Coping with belongings
- ❑ HANDOUT 14:   Questions & comments
- ❑ HANDOUT 15:   Grief types
- ❑ HANDOUT 16:   RESILIENCE RX: Sleep well
- ❑ HANDOUT 17:   Bible work

SESSION 4: FACING OUR FEARS

- ❑ HANDOUT 18:   Coping with fear
- ❑ HANDOUT 19:   Why grief robs our memory
- ❑ HANDOUT 20:   Remembering the details
- ❑ HANDOUT 21:   A letter to family & friends
- ❑ HANDOUT 22:   RESILIENCE RX: Chromotherapy
- ❑ HANDOUT 23:   Bible work

SESSION 5: COPING WITH DATES & HOLIDAYS

- ❏ HANDOUT 24:   Coping with painful dates
- ❏ HANDOUT 25:   Coping with holidays
- ❏ HANDOUT 26:   Tips for supporters
- ❏ HANDOUT 27:   12 Nights of Kindness
- ❏ HANDOUT 28:   RESILIENCE RX: Music therapy
- ❏ HANDOUT 29:   Bible work

SESSION 6: LIFE, DEATH & FAITH

- ❏ HANDOUT 30:   What do I believe?
- ❏ HANDOUT 31:   The purpose of life
- ❏ HANDOUT 32:   Faith & Death
- ❏ HANDOUT 33:   God's script
- ❏ HANDOUT 34:   RESILIENCE RX: Dance/movement therapy
- ❏ HANDOUT 35:   Bible work

SESSION 7: FINDING COMFORT

- ❏ HANDOUT 36:   Finding comfort
- ❏ HANDOUT 37:   Collateral blessings
- ❏ HANDOUT 38:   Finding an outlet
- ❏ HANDOUT 39:   Why giving is good for the giver
- ❏ HANDOUT 40:   RESILIENCE RX: Laugh therapy
- ❏ HANDOUT 41:   Bible work

SESSION 8: FINDING HOPE

- ❏ HANDOUT 42:   Is hope possible after loss?
- ❏ HANDOUT 43:   The power of gratitude
- ❏ HANDOUT 44:   My playbook of grief
- ❏ HANDOUT 45:   When grief steals our Technicolor
- ❏ HANDOUT 46:   Turning pain into purpose
- ❏ HANDOUT 47:   What now?
- ❏ HANDOUT 48:   RESILIENCE RX: Hug therapy
- ❏ HANDOUT 49:   Bible work

SESSIONS

SESSION 1

LOSS & GRIEF

SESSION FORMAT

This first session is an introduction to the next 8 weeks. Following is this session's format:

1. Welcome and short introduction of facilitator(s)
2. Review of housekeeping details
3. Explanation of the process
4. Review of the ground rules
5. Review importance of homework
6. Introduction of participants
7. Emotional check-in
8. Bible work check-in
9. Introduction of session topic
10. Review of self care
11. Conclusion

Each session hereafter will begin with an emotional check-in, offer a topic for discussion, questions to guide the facilitators, and finish with homework recap. Check the boxes as you go to stay on track.

LET'S BEGIN

1. OPEN THE MEETING

❑ Open with the prayer on page 26 or one of your own, if desired, then welcome everyone and thank them for investing in themselves by being there.

❑ Introduce yourself by sharing the details below. If you have a co-facilitator, allow him/her to introduce themselves. By sharing your own personal loss experience, you reassure participants that you speak a loss language and understand the grief journey from your perspective. For the sake of time, keep it under 60 seconds.

FORMS & HANDOUTS

❑ **FORM**: My Participants
❑ **FORM**: Blank registrations for latecomers
❑ **FORM**: Sign-in sheet
❑ **HANDOUT 1**: Ground rules
❑ **HANDOUT 2**: Reacting to Loss
❑ **HANDOUT 3**: Grief stages
❑ **HANDOUT 4**: A word about resilience
❑ **HANDOUT 5**: Resilience Rx: Caring plan
❑ **HANDOUT 6**: Benefits of journaling
❑ **HANDOUT 7**: Bible work

MATERIALS

❑ Workbooks
❑ Handouts
❑ Notebook & pen
❑ Nametags
❑ Tissue
❑ Community resources
❑ Refreshments

Details to include in your introduction:

1. Name and credentials (if any)
2. Where you're from and how long you've lived in the area
3. The first name of your own deceased loved one and your relationship to him/her
4. The age and year of his/her death
5. The cause of death

2. REVIEW HOUSEKEEPING

❑ Briefly review the following facility details and expectations:
1. Location of the restrooms and garbage cans
2. Where to put the chairs when not in use
3. Any facility rules that must be followed during the session

3. DISCUSS HOMEWORK EXPECTATIONS

❑ Explain that each session of the grief support group is part of a two-fold process:
1. Attending each session is the first part
2. Homework by way of Bible work and a self-care exercise are the second part

❑ Explain that both self-care and Bible work are important parts of griefwork. It holds one accountable for being proactive in their own grief journey, and offers an opportunity to deepen the understanding of what they're experiencing in an environment where they feel comfortable and safe. Remind participants that the more they invest in this process, the more they'll understand their own grief journey, and benefit from the support group.

❑ Share with participants that research shows that penning our deepest emotions through journaling helps to reduce stress and improve our mood. By expressing oneself in a safe, private space, difficult emotions become less overwhelming. Given that griefwork is largely working through emotions, journaling is especially useful for those who tend to push their emotions away. **Ask participants to review the Bible prompts in their workbook and journal at least once between sessions.** Encourage them to review the Bible for scriptures that reasonate, and then write about it. Additionally, they can write a letter to God. They need not share what they write, it's merely a supportive exercise for their eyes only.

❑ Handouts not included in the session discussions can be read at home by participants in their own time.

4. REVIEW GROUND RULES

❑ Using the Ground Rules handout, review ground rules for expectations and ask everyone for their verbal agreement before moving forward.

5. INVITE EACH PARTICIPANT TO INTRODUCE THEMSELVES

To help participants become familiar with one another, allow each one to introduce him/herself by answering the questions below.

❑ What's your name and where are you from?

❑ What's the first name of your deceased loved one and your relationship to him/her?

❑ What's the age and year of his/her death?

❑ How did s/he die?

❑ Have you participated in a grief support group before?

6. EMOTIONAL CHECK-IN

An emotional check-in allows participants to acknowledge and verbalize what they're feeling or struggling with most in that moment. In doing so, they learn to validate their emotions. It also affords participants an opportunity to release emotional steam before actively participating in the support group.

❑ At the beginning of each session, go around the circle and ask participants one at a time the following question: "**If you could choose one word to describe your emotions today, what would you choose and why?**"

❑ Keep the check-in short, about 30 to 60 seconds per participant.

❑ Thank each participant for sharing before moving on to the next participant.

7. BIBLE WORK CHECK-IN

Although Bible work will be done at home, you'll invite participants to share anything they wish in relation to their Bible work. Perhaps it's a scripture they discovered that really resonated within, or a short passage from their journaling.

❑ Just like with the emotional check-in, beginning with session 2, go around the circle and ask participants one at a time the following question: "**How did your Bible work go? Is there anything you wish to share?**"

❑ Keep the check-in short, about 30 to 60 seconds per participant.

❑ Thank each participant for sharing before moving on to the next participant.

NOTE: It's okay if the emotional check-in and/or Bible work check-in go longer, just be mindful that the more time spent on those discussions, the less time the group will have for the main discussion. As a facilitator, this can be a balancing act, depending on the needs of the group for that session. If a lengthy discussion ensues about emotions or Bible work, allow the conversation to continue in that direction for a bit before moving on to the main discussion.

8. **DISCUSSION**: **Loss & Grief**

❑ **LOSS.** Because the grief journey is unique as one's fingerprint, invite participants to explore and externalize their own grief reactions. Using the handout **REACTING TO LOSS**, guide the discussion around the circle by asking, **"Which reactions to your loss has been hardest for you?"** Allow each participant to answer then thank him/her for sharing before moving on to the next participant.

❑ **GRIEF.** Grief stages are theories only. Invite participants to share what they thought the grief journey would be like compared to how it actually is for each of them. Using the handout **GRIEF STAGES**, guide the discussion around the circle by asking each participant, **"What was your belief about the stages of grief, and where do you feel you are on your journey now?"** Allow each participant to answer then thank him/her for sharing before moving on to the next participant.

9. **RESILIENCE RX**

Explain the importance of self-care, especially when grieving. Share with participants that developing a self-care plan is an important tool that will help them tend to their own physical, emotional and spiritual needs, and will help reduce stress by doing things that trigger endorphins to counteract stress hormones.

❑ Encourage participants to create a self-care plan and explore one new addition each week using the Resilience Rx™ strategies in the workbook.

10. **CONCLUSION**

Thank participants for coming and investing in their own well-being. Encourage them to read or review the handouts, journal their thoughts, and create a self-care plan. If desired, you can end each session with a poem, prayer, or group hug.

WHY DO WE THANK EACH PARTICIPANT FOR SHARING?

Thanking each participant for sharing his/her emotions and thoughts before moving on to the next participant serves three purposes:

1. It acknowledges that the speaking participant was heard.

2. It validates their contribution without judgment, and signals acceptance of—and respect for—what they shared.

3. It signals to the participant that you're moving on to the next participant. This cue helps participants to avoid talking over one another.

SESSION 1 | HANDOUT 1

GROUND RULES

A grief support group is an important part of griefwork. By being here and actively participating in this safe environment, you'll learn to better understand your emotions, gain coping skills, and make new friends. In short, active participation will reward you in the end. To help the group run smoothly and be a process that benefits everyone, it's imperative for everyone to understand and agree to the etiquette rules below.

CONFIDENTIALTIY

Nobody likes to be the brunt of gossip. To help fellow participants feel safe when divulging personal emotions and experiences, **keep what you hear confidential**. This confidentiality also extends to personal information.

ADVICE

This support group is about sharing emotions and experiences, not advice. While it's human nature to try to help others, advice can be unwelcome, even if we think it's helpful. **Please refrain from giving advice, or starting any sentence with, "You should . . . ".**

JUDGMENT

When we judge someone's reaction or thought process, we imply superiority. Acceptance of our differences and respect for one another's opinion is critical to our own learning. Seek to understand rather than persuade. **Suspend judgment during group sessions.**

PROFANITY

Offensive language isn't necessary to get one's point across. To be sensitive to those around you, **please refrain from using profanity and slurs.**

LISTENING

Holding the space for one another and listening is as important as speaking. Active listening helps us learn from one another. When we're not listening, we rob ourselves of an opportunity to understand and learn new insights. **Please refrain from interrupting or having side discussions. Also, please turn off cell phone ringers unless it's critical for it to be on.**

SENSITIVITY

One's perspective is influenced by beliefs and experiences. Appreciate the value of people who share a different belief, and **be respectful of their experiences.**

HONESTY

Honesty is the foundation of this support group. When one isn't being honest, they cause others to question their own experiences and emotions. When we are honest about our own emotions and struggles, we validate our own experience. **Speak from the heart about your experiences.**

H01/GROUND RULES

REACTING TO LOSS

Not all people respond the same way to death of a loved one. The emotional impact depends on a number of factors including inner resilience, personality, adverse childhood experiences, and availability of support through family, friends, and coworkers. Some have more severe, longer lasting reactions.

Further, grief is not just an emotional response. Though the nature and scope of grief differs, common reactions occur in 6 distinct categories.

☑ Cognitive   ☑ Physical
☑ Emotional   ☑ Social
☑ Behavioral   ☑ spiritual

NORMAL COGNITIVE REACTIONS

- Forgetfulness
- Poor concentration
- Low productivity
- Negative Attitude
- Confusion
- Guilt
- Preoccupation with loss event

NORMAL BEHAVIORAL REACTIONS

- 1000-yard stare
- Sleep disturbance
- Crying spells
- Lashing out
- Resentment
- Hyper-startle
- Increased risk taking

NORMAL EMOTIONAL REACTIONS

- Disbelief
- Shock
- Anxiety
- Frustration and/or irritability
- Mood swings
- Temper outbursts
- Nightmares
- Crying spells

NORMAL PHYSICAL REACTIONS

- Appetite change
- Fatigue
- Headaches
- Insomnia
- Restlessness
- Upset stomach/nausea
- Weight change

NORMAL SPIRITUAL REACTIONS

- Anger at God
- Emptiness
- Doubt
- Loss of direction
- Cynicism
- Cessation from practice of faith

NORMAL SOCIAL REACTIONS

- Change in friendships
- Change in career or workplace
- Altered status (going from married to single)
- Loss of motivation
- Withdrawal from family and friends

ANSWER THE FOLLOWING QUESTIONS

Which cognitive reaction has been hardest for you to manage?

ANSWER:

Which behavioral reaction has been hardest for you to manage?

ANSWER:

Which emotional reaction has been hardest for you to manage?

ANSWER:

Which physical reaction has hit you hardest?

ANSWER:

Which spiritual reaction has been hardest for you to manage?

ANSWER:

Which social reaction has been hardest for you to manage?

ANSWER:

SESSION 1 | HANDOUT 3

GRIEF STAGES

Grief models

Over the years, researchers have created various grief models in an effort to help clinicians and practitioners better understand what cognitive, social and emotional challenges their clients commonly experience. Although each model has its own parameters based on theories, it's important to remember that theories are concepts only, and grief remains as unique as a fingerprint. Below are some of those models and the prongs of their theory.

DUAL PROCESS

DR. MARGARET STROEBE & DR. HENK SCHUT

- Loss orientation
- Restoration orientation

FOUR TASKS OF MOURNING

DR. J. WILLIAM WORDEN

- To accept the reality of the loss
- To work through the pain of grief
- To adjust to life without the deceased
- To maintain a connection to the deceased while moving on with life

SIX R PROCESSES OF MOURNING

DR. THERESE RANDO

- Recognize
- React
- Recollect
- Relinquish
- Readjust
- Reinvest

A NOTE ABOUT THE 5 STAGES OF GRIEF

Death and dying pioneer Dr. Elisabeth Kübler-Ross wrote the 5-stage model for terminally ill patients who were dying, not for their surviving family. It's not clear exactly when the model was applied to those in mourning, yet the concept stuck.

Because many mourners still believe their grief will follow a 5-stage process, they become confused as to why it isn't happening in such a simple, linear path, leaving some to believe they're "failing" grief. Most of us will experience grief in many different stages, some of which even occur at the same time. It's important to remember that we all experience grief in our own way.

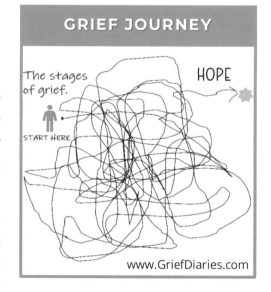

SESSION 1 | HANDOUT 4

A WORD ABOUT RESILIENCE

WHAT IS RESILIENCE?

Resilience is the ability to adapt to life difficulties—including loss of a loved one. Building resilience through strategies that support the brain, body, and emotions during difficult times can help reduce the damaging effects of grief.

THE GOAL

The goal of Resilience Rx™ handouts is to offer easy evidence-based self-help techniques that trigger positive hormones—dopamine, serotonin, and oxytocin—to offset stress, and support you as you learn to move forward with your loved one in your heart instead of your arms.

HOW DO YOU STRENGTHEN RESILIENCE?

The first step is to take good care of yourself. We can't always predict loss and other stressors, but practicing self-help techniques that tend to our physical, mental, emotional, and spiritual needs can help anchor and strengthen our ability to weather times of upheaval.

There are multiple ways to trigger positive hormones. Use the Resilience Rx™ evidence-based modalities in this workbook as a resource for adding tools to your self-care toolbox. Doing so will help lift your spirit and soothe your heart when mourning the loss of someone you love.

RESILIENCE RX TIP 1

CREATE YOUR CARE PLAN

WHAT TO KNOW

> Research shows that when you feel better, you cope better.

Losing someone we love changes how we live and who we are. The first step is to take good care of yourself. Self-care refers to healthy habits and activities that reduce stress by doing things that activate endorphins—our happy hormones—dopamine, oxytocin, and serotonin, to counteract stress hormones.

WHY IT MATTERS

Grief is a significant stressor that impacts our mental, physical, and emotional health. Self-care can improve our well-being, minimize stress, reduce the damaging effects of grief, and help us adjust as we learn to live with our loved one in our heart instead of our arms.

Creating a self-care plan that tends to your physical, emotional, social, and spiritual needs will help strengthen your inner resilience when juggling the demands of life while grieving, and can help anchor your ability to weather times of upheaval in the future. By identify things you enjoy, you'll be able to create a unique and helpful self-care plan you're more likely to stick with.

AIMS OF SELF CARE

Grief can make us feel out of control. Self-care helps to restore some of that control through managing our health and well-being. When we feel physically and spiritually stronger, our coping improves. Self-care can:

- Help manage stress
- Prevent physical illness
- Help maintain equilibrium and honor one's own needs

HOW TO BEGIN

1. Identify your emotional, physical, social and spiritual needs.
2. Create your self-care plan and fill it with activities you enjoy. Use Resilience Rx™ tips in this manual to help.
3. Put it into action and stick to it.
4. Reassess it every 3 months and adjust as needed.

Starting now, create a plan that tends to your emotional, physical, social and spiritual needs, and promise to do activities that activate your brain's happy hormones.

HOW TO CREATE YOUR PLAN

Use the suggestions under each heading below to help formulate a self-care plan you can stick with.

PHYSICAL NEEDS

Nourishing your body will help you feel better. When you feel better, you cope better.

- ✓ Practice good sleep hygiene
- ✓ Engage in light exercise, housekeeping or dancing to keep the body moving
- ✓ Stay hydrated and eat for health
- ✓ Make time for restorative relaxation
- ✓ Enjoy a good belly laugh each day

MY PHYSICAL GOALS:

☐ _____
☐ _____
☐ _____
☐ _____
☐ _____
☐ _____

EMOTIONAL NEEDS

Our emotional needs are met through understanding, empathy, and support.

- ✓ Surround yourself with others who speak your loss language
- ✓ Talk to loved ones about your loss
- ✓ Express your emotions in a journal
- ✓ Engage in enjoyable outlets such as coloring, knitting, gardening, puzzles, etc.

MY EMOTIONAL GOALS:

☐ _____
☐ _____
☐ _____
☐ _____
☐ _____
☐ _____

SOCIAL NEEDS

Fulfilling engagements and interactions help guard against depression and isolation.

- ✓ Develop supportive friendships
- ✓ Volunteer in the community
- ✓ Take or teach a self-enrichment class
- ✓ Join a book, tennis, quilt or knitting club
- ✓ Travel

MY SOCIAL GOALS:

☐ _____
☐ _____
☐ _____
☐ _____
☐ _____
☐ _____

SPIRITUAL NEEDS

Our spiritual needs are met through inner reflection.

- ✓ Each day write down one thing you're grateful for, or try Bible journaling
- ✓ Engage in a reflective practice such as prayer, meditation or yoga
- ✓ Talk to clergy or a spiritual mentor

MY SPIRITUAL GOALS:

☐ _____
☐ _____
☐ _____
☐ _____
☐ _____
☐ _____

BENEFITS OF JOURNALING

BENEFITS

Journaling is an opportunity to externalize one's emotions, struggles, frustrations and triumphs. It's especially useful for those who push their emotions away. By expressing them in a safe, contained space, difficult emotions become less overwhelming and easier to manage. Further, the repetitive hand motion required to write induces a meditative state, calming our mind and emotions.

As part of your griefwork, learn to keep a Bible journal as part of your caring plan.

HELPFUL HINTS

✓ Write whatever comes to mind without censoring yourself.

✓ Keep it honest.

✓ God isn't looking for perfect. Don't worry about editing, grammar, vocabulary or punctuation. Just put pen to paper to externalize your thoughts, emotions, experiences, or anything you want to vent about.

✓ Journal for at least 5 minutes at a time. Set a timer if needed.

✓ A journal is for your eyes only. If you keep it confidential, you're more likely to be brutally honest. Keep it private unless you wish to share it with someone you trust.

✓ Consider keeping your journal for the long haul. Revisiting it can help you continue to process your grief, and often becomes an opportunity to recognize how far you've come.

PROMPTS TO HELP YOU BEGIN

If you get stuck and the words just won't come, write a letter to God, or use the prompts on page 181 or the prompts below to begin, and then let your heart guide the pen from there.

> **WHAT TO KNOW**
>
> Research shows that penning your deepest emotions helps to reduce stress and improve one's mood.

❏ This is what happened today . . . .

❏ I'm experiencing these feelings about it . . . .

❏ I'm thinking these thoughts . . . .

❏ I'm most fearful of . . . .

❏ I'm struggling with this emotion the most right now . . . .

❏ I wish others knew this about my journey . . . .

❏ I'm most angry at . . . .

❏ I'm grateful for . . .

SESSION 1 | HANDOUT 7

BIBLE WORK

What does the Bible say about death?

Blessed are those who mourn,
for they shall be comforted.

MATTHEW 5:4

SCRIPTURES TO EXPLORE

- ❑ PSALM 34:18
- ❑ PSALM 55:22
- ❑ ECCLESIASTES 3:1-22
- ❑ 1 THESSALONIANS 4:13-17

The Christian view of death is special. The belief in God, resurrected Jesus, salvation, heaven and the eternity of the human spirit encourages hope in time of despair.

Some believe once we die, we simply cease existing. The Bible says differently. And yet, because we're human with human emotions, believing in one's salvation doesn't erase the depth of grief we feel over such a profound loss. Life inevitably includes sorrow, sometimes accompanied by bitterness and hopelessness. God gave us tears to express our grief.

Ecclesiastes speaks about the seasons of life. Much like the dead of winter is necessary for plants to regrow from the roots up, pain and sorrow often lead to necessary growth of our soul. So, while Christians aren't immune to sorrow, does the Bible's view of everlasting life ease our grief?

HOW DOES THE BIBLE PORTRAY DEATH? HOW DO YOU FEEL ABOUT THIS?

Does the Bible's portrayal of death bring you comfort? What scriptures do you find helpful?

ANSWER:

MY SCRIPTURES

Be the light
Ephesians 5:8

PRAYER

Dear God,

I am overwhelmed by this season of grief. My heart is fractured like broken shards. I thank you for the precious gift of my loved one's life, yet I am unsure how to manage without their physical presence.

Lord, please wrap your loving arms around me and give me the strength to get through today, and remind my heart that you will carry me through this dark time. Thank you for hearing my cries, Lord.

In Jesus' name I pray, Amen.

J21/WHAT DOES THE BIBLE SAY ABOUT DEATH

A LETTER TO GOD

TODAY'S DATE: _____

Dear God,

iCare

SESSION 2

COPING WITH TRIGGERS

IC02/SESSION 2 INSTRUCTIONS

SESSION FORMAT

This session focuses on understanding triggers, secondary losses, and grief myths that remain a stronghold in society. Learning to recognize as a group how these affect us individually can facilitate a meaningful discussion about shared coping strategies.

Following is this session's format:

1. Welcome and opening of session
2. Quick review of ground rules
3. Emotional check-in
4. Bible work check-in
5. Topic discussion
6. Review of self care
7. Conclusion

FACILITATION REMINDERS:

✓ Keep conversation moving. Protect conversation from being monopolized.

✓ Ensure every participant has an opportunity to answer the question. If the conversation jumps around the circle, be sure to circle back to those participants who haven't yet answered.

✓ If tension or disagreements flare during the discussion, reminder participants that this is a judgment-free zone and all perspectives are welcome.

✓ Stay neutral yet supportive.

LET'S BEGIN

1. **OPEN THE MEETING.**

   ❏ Ask everyone to take a seat, open with the prayer on page 26 or one of your own, if desired, then welcome them back to session #2. Remind them that they are investing in their future by being there.

   ❏ Perform a quick review of the ground rules as a friendly reminder of expectations.

FORMS & HANDOUTS

❏ **FORM:** My Participants
❏ **FORM:** Blank registrations for latecomers
❏ **FORM:** Sign-in sheet
❏ **HANDOUT 8:** Coping with triggers
❏ **HANDOUT 9:** Ripple effect
❏ **HANDOUT 10:** Societal myths about loss
❏ **HANDOUT 11:** Resilience Rx: Sensory therapy
❏ **HANDOUT 12:** Bible work

MATERIALS

❏ Workbooks
❏ Handouts
❏ Notebook & pen
❏ Nametags (if needed)
❏ Tissue
❏ Community resources
❏ Refreshments

2. EMOTIONAL CHECK-IN

❑ Going around the circle, ask participants one at a time the following question: "**If you could choose one word to describe your emotions today, what would you choose and why?**" Keep it short by limiting answers to about 30 to 60 seconds each. Thank each participant for sharing before moving on to the next participant.

3. BIBLE WORK

❑ Going around the circle, invite participants to share a quick recap of how they did with their bible work by asking the following question, **"How did you do with your Bible scriptures and journaling?"** Keep it short by limiting answers to about 30 to 60 seconds each. Thank each participant for sharing before moving on to the next participant.

❑ Encourage participants to continue reading the Bible and journaling as part of their griefwork.

4. DISCUSSION: **Coping with triggers**

❑ **TRIGGERS.** Because triggers are unique to each of us, invite participants to explore and externalize which triggers are currently hardest to manage. Using the handout **COPING WITH TRIGGERS,** guide the discussion by asking, **"Which triggers do you find are the hardest to manage?"** Allow each participant to answer then thank him/her for sharing before moving on to the next participant.

❑ **RIPPLE EFFECT.** Primary losses often result in secondary losses. Using the handout **RIPPLE EFFECT**, guide the discussion by asking, **"What secondary losses have been unexpectedly hardest for you?"** Allow each participant to answer then thank him/her for sharing before moving on to the next participant.

5. RESILIENCE RX

❑ Remind participants of the importance of self-care as part of their griefwork. Going around the circle, invite participants to share how they did with creating their care plan by asking the following question, **"How did you do with your care plans?"**

❑ Invite them to review this session's handout and consider including it in their care plan.

6. CONCLUSION

Thank participants for coming and investing in their own well-being. Encourage them to:
❑ Read or review the session handouts
❑ Continue Bible work and journaling
❑ Add one activity to their self-care plan
❑ If desired, you can end with a poem, prayer, or group hug

COPING WITH TRIGGERS

WHAT ARE GRIEF TRIGGERS?

Grief can be triggered by anything that brings up memories related to our loss. They are little reminders that throw us back in time and ambush our emotions, causing anxiety and/or an emotional outburst.

WHAT TO KNOW

Because grief is unique as a fingerprint, triggers are highly individualized. For example, two parents who lost the same child may experience different triggers. Why? Because each parent has a unique personality, filters, and childhood experiences, and each had a unique relationship with that child. All of these individual components will dictate each parent's individual triggers. What to know:

☑ People experiencing the same loss may not have the same triggers

☑ Triggers may or may not lessen with time

☑ Triggers may be subtle or surprising

TRIGGER EXAMPLES

☑ **Music.** Studies show a link between music and memory. Certain songs can evoke joy or sadness. They also stimulate memories, transporting us back in time to emotional events. While one particular song might be triggering now, it's important to know that one day that same song might also bring comfort when your emotions aren't so raw.

☑ **Smells or sounds**. Scents and sounds also play a role in our memories, linking our experiences with our deceased loved one. Smells such as a flower, perfume, even cigarettes can hijack our emotions. Sounds such as a particular ring tone or the sound of a siren can be especially triggering.

☑ **Lost opportunities.** Lost opportunities often serve as a reminder of our deceased loved one's absence and/or evokes a feel-ing of having been robbed of that experience. For instance, when a friend's son weds, a grieving parent might feel robbed that they'll never see their own child walk down the aisle. When a widow or widower has their first grandchild, they are both overjoyed yet sad that their beloved will never get to hold the new little one.

☑ **Sights.** The sight of certain things such as a hospital, a certain color, someone's hair, or even something as simple as a school bus can trigger a wave of grief.

☑ **Special days.** Grief can be especially tender during cyclical or special calendar days, such as favorite holidays, birthdays, death or wedding anniversaries, etc. Even a particular season such as spring can be triggering.

iCare

HOW TO COPE

Coping with grief triggers is best managed by identifying your triggers, then proactively managing them. For instance, if a certain restaurant is triggering, avoid that restaurant for the time being. It doesn't mean you need to avoid it for the rest of your life . . . what is painful today may bring you comfort tomorrow. But for now, avoid potentially triggering situations until the rawness has softened.

- Identify your current triggers

- When you're triggered, reassure yourself that, in this moment, you are safe

- Remind yourself to breathe through the nose and exhale through the mouth

- Comfort yourself as best you can using your tactile senses, such as holding a soft blanket

- Consider removing yourself from the situation if possible

- Engage in an activity you love to help trigger endorphins and calm fear

- Avoid minimizing the trigger's significance even if you don't understand it

ANSWER THE FOLLOWING QUESTIONS

Name some triggers you're currently experiencing in your grief journey.

- ❏ _____
- ❏ _____
- ❏ _____
- ❏ _____
- ❏ _____
- ❏ _____

Name some things you can do to help yourself manage current triggers.

- ❏ _____
- ❏ _____
- ❏ _____
- ❏ _____
- ❏ _____

RIPPLE EFFECT

SECONDARY LOSSES

Death has a ripple effect in that the death of a loved one is a primary loss that often results in secondary losses. While the initial death event is often public, many secondary losses are less obvious and go unobserved by outsiders.

Some of the secondary losses might include:

LOSS OF FAMILY STRUCTURE

- o A widow who now lives alone and has to manage all the household responsibilities.
- o A child who lost a parent and now lives in a single parent household.
- o A child who lost a sibling also lost a playmate.

LOSS OF IDENTITY

- o When an only child dies, a parent often questions whether they are still a mother or a father.
- o When a sibling loses a twin, s/he now has to navigate life as a singlet.
- o When a spouse dies, the widow/widower must adjust from being half of a pair to being alone.

LOSS OF LIFESTYLE

- o Loss of financial security.
- o Loss of a planned future.
- o A parent who volunteered for a deceased child's team or activity often loses that connection.
- o A child who loses a deceased sibling's friends.
- o A widow who has to adjust to being single again, and often is forced to find support outside his/her married friends.

ANSWER THE FOLLOWING QUESTION

Have you experienced any secondary losses since your primary loss? If so, list them here.

- ❑ _____
- ❑ _____
- ❑ _____
- ❑ _____

SOCIETAL MYTHS ABOUT LOSS

Death and grief have been around since the beginning of mankind, and yet grief remains a taboo topic in many societies. This lack of understanding can lead many mourners to feel as though s/he is a square peg in a round world, no longer fitting in. Because grief can also be stigmatizing, mourners hesitate to educate family and friends with facts. Following are common myths that have a stronghold.

MYTH: Grief ends after one year.
FACT: The bereavement timeline is unique to every individual, and many grieve in subtle ways for the rest of their life. Accepting a societal timeline can lead to disappointment.

MYTH: People who mourn for more than a year are just looking for sympathy.
FACT: Crying is a healthy response to emotional pain. Suppressed grief leads to complications. It's critically important that mourners be allowed to cry as part of the process for as long as they need.

MYTH: Time heals all wounds.
FACT: While the rawness of loss can soften with time, the rate at which we reconcile our loss largely depends upon the griefwork we do along the way. If we ignore the wound, it remains unchanged.

MYTH: Grief is just an emotional response.
FACT: Experiencing a first-degree loss affects far more than just our emotions. It can affect many facets of our life, including our behaveioral, cognitive, emotional, physical, and spiritual self.

MYTH: Women grieve more than men.
FACT: While the male and female brains are wired differently, males grieve just as deeply as females, though they tend to externalize it through physical reactions instead of emotional reactions.

MYTH: There are 5 grief stages.
FACT: In 1969, Dr. Elisabeth Kübler-Ross theorized five stages of grief that terminal patients facing death often go through. Loved ones left behind can experience many stages, and the timeline isn't linear.

MYTH: Grief and mourning are the same thing.
FACT: Grief is our response to losing a loved one. Mourning is how a person expresses their grief, such as choosing to wear black clothing or getting a memorial tattoo.

MYTH: Lack of tears means a mourner has moved on and is okay.
FACT: Crying is one way we express sorrow. Mourners react and express grief in many ways.

MYTH: The first year of grief is the hardest.
FACT: Many mourners find the second year of grief to be harder than the first. This is due in large part to the numbness wearing off and the reality settling in. Some find that grief eventually eases as the rawness softens.

SESSION 2 | HANDOUT 11

RESILIENCE RX TIP 2

SENSORY THERAPY

Our five senses play a role in how we feel and can be influenced by what our senses take in. Treating ourselves to something that evokes sensorial joy stimulates our brain to release feel-good hormones that help offset grief hormones. While the joy we feel doesn't minimize the grief, it reminds our body that not all pleasure is lost.

HOW IT WORKS

The sensation of pleasure triggers our brain to release happy hormones—endorphins—such as oxytocin, dopamine, and serotonin.

RULE OF 5s

Every day practice the Rule of 5s by enjoying the following:

- 5 things you can **see**
- 4 things you can **touch**
- 3 things you can **hear**
- 2 things you can **smell**
- 1 thing you can **taste**

Practice the Rule of 5s below to give yourself some form of sensory pleasure every day. With practice, the awareness and perception of delight eventually becomes effortless, and is an important step toward restoring balance after loss.

SIGHT—VISUAL SUGGESTIONS:

- ♦ Watch a sunrise or sunset
- ♦ Look at a cherished photo or a favorite memento
- ♦ Use a plant or flowers to enliven your work space
- ♦ Enjoy the beauty of a garden, the beach, a park, or your own backyard
- ♦ Surround yourself with colors that lift your spirits

TACTILE—TOUCH SUGGESTIONS:

- ♦ Soak in a warm tub with Epsom salts or bath oil
- ♦ Wear a pair of extra soft socks
- ♦ Wrap yourself in a soft scarf or blanket
- ♦ Pet a dog or cat
- ♦ Hold a stuffed animal
- ♦ Walk barefoot on cool grass

THINGS I CAN SEE THAT BRING ME JOY

- ☐ _____
- ☐ _____
- ☐ _____
- ☐ _____
- ☐ _____

THINGS I CAN TOUCH THAT BRING ME JOY

- ☐ _____
- ☐ _____
- ☐ _____
- ☐ _____
- ☐ _____

HEARING—SOUND SUGGESTIONS:

♦ Listen to relaxing or upbeat music

♦ Listen to laughter on YouTube or comedy show

♦ Listen to a water feature such as the sound of the ocean, a fountain, a waterfall or the rain

♦ Hang a birdfeeder and listen to the singsong

♦ Listen to happy noises at a park

♦ Hang windchimes near a window

THINGS I CAN HEAR THAT BRING ME JOY

☐ _____

☐ _____

☐ _____

☐ _____

☐ _____

OLFACTION—SMELL SUGGESTIONS:

♦ Shower or bathe with a lovely scented soap

♦ Light a fragrant candle or burn incense

♦ Apply a scented lotion to your skin before bed

♦ Buy a fragrant flower bouquet for the kitchen or your office

♦ Experiment with different essential oils in a diffuser

♦ Spritz on your favorite perfume

THINGS I CAN SMELL THAT BRING ME JOY

☐ _____

☐ _____

☐ _____

☐ _____

☐ _____

GUSTATION—TASTE SUGGESTIONS:

♦ Enjoy an icy cold beverage

♦ Enjoy a mug of herbal tea

♦ Enjoy hot cocoa with whipped cream

♦ Chew flavored gum

♦ Indulge in a piece of dark chocolate

♦ Enjoy a ripe piece of fruit

♦ Eat a minty candy

THINGS I CAN TASTE THAT BRINGS ME JOY

☐ _____

☐ _____

☐ _____

☐ _____

☐ _____

SESSION 2 | HANDOUT 12

BIBLE WORK

What does the Bible say about grief?

Rejoice with those who rejoice,
and weep with those who weep.

ROMANS 12:15

SCRIPTURES TO EXPLORE

- ☐ PSALM 34:17-19
- ☐ 2 SAMUEL 12:16-23
- ☐ JOHN 14:1-6

The story of Jacob's loss of Joseph, his favorite son, told in **Genesis 37**, reveals Jacob's struggle with inconsolable grief.

Isaiah 53 tells of the purpose of God's Son, Jesus Christ, bearing our transgressions and grief on our behalf. The New Testament proclaims promise, hope, relief and salvation from the grief, pain and suffering that fills our life.

While the Bible permits us to grieve, how do we effectively cope with grief, and what wisdom does the Bible offer in guiding us?

WHAT DOES THE BIBLE SAY ABOUT GRIEVING THE DEATH OF A LOVED ONE?

Does the Bible's portrayal of grief and mourning bring you comfort? If so, what scriptures do you find helpful?

ANSWER:

MY SCRIPTURES

Be the light

Ephesians 5:8

PRAYER

Dear God,

My heart and soul are weary from the grief and upheaval. All the joy has gone from my world and I'm unable to see the end of this journey. Lord, please give me hope that peace is waiting for me, that this journey through sorrow is but only a chapter.

Lord, I thank you for the precious gift of eternal life, yet my grief remains all consuming. I ask you to help me keep my eyes on you, and help me feel your presence as a reminder that I am not alone in my season of grief. Thank you for hearing my cries, Lord.

In Jesus' name I pray, Amen.

A LETTER TO GOD

TODAY'S DATE: _____

Dear God,

iCare

J29/A LETTER TO GOD

SESSION 3

GRIEF STRESS

IC03/SESSION 3 INSTRUCTIONS

SESSION FORMAT

This session focuses on some of the secondary grief stress-ors such as addressing our loved one's belongings, and the hurtful things well-meaning people sometimes say. By addressing these painful moments in the safety of the group, mourners feel less alone and can even learn from one another about how to cope with such situations.

Following is this session's format:

1. Welcome and opening of session
2. Emotional check-in
3. Bible work check-in
4. Topic discussion
5. Review of self care
6. Conclusion

FACILITATION REMINDERS:

✓ Keep conversation moving. Protect conversation from being monopolized.

✓ Ensure every participant has an opportunity to answer the question. If the conversation jumps around the circle, be sure to circle back to those participants who haven't yet answered.

✓ If tension or disagreements flare during the discussion, reminder participants that this is a judgment-free zone and all perspectives are welcome.

✓ Stay neutral yet supportive.

LET'S BEGIN

1. **OPEN THE MEETING.**

   Ask everyone to take a seat, open with the prayer on page 26 or one of your own, if desired, and then welcome them back to session #3. Thank them for investing in their future by being there.

FORMS & HANDOUTS

☐ **FORM**: My Participants
☐ **FORM**: Sign-in sheet
☐ **HANDOUT 13**: Coping with belongings
☐ **HANDOUT 14**: Questions & comments
☐ **HANDOUT 15**: Grief types
☐ **HANDOUT 16**: Resilience Rx: Sleep well
☐ **HANDOUT 17**: Bible work

MATERIALS

☐ Workbooks
☐ Handouts
☐ Notebook & pen
☐ Nametags (if needed)
☐ Tissue
☐ Community resources
☐ Refreshments

2. **EMOTIONAL CHECK-IN**

❏ Going around the circle, ask participants one at a time the following question: "**If you could choose one word to describe your emotions today, what would you choose and why?**" Keep it short by limiting answers to about 30 to 60 seconds each. Thank each participant for sharing before moving on to the next participant.

3. **BIBLE WOK**

❏ Going around the circle, invite participants to share a quick recap of how they did with their bible work by asking the following question, **"How did you do with your Bible scriptures and journaling?"** Keep it short by limiting answers to 30 to 60 seconds each. Thank each participant for sharing before moving on to the next participant.

❏ Encourage participants to continue reading the Bible and journaling as part of their griefwork.

4. **DISCUSSION: Grief stress**

❏ **BELONGINGS.** Because coping with a deceased loved one's belongings can be a sensitive topic for mourners, invite participants to externalize how they dealt with their loved one's belongings. Using the handout **COPING WITH BELONGINGS,** guide the discussion by asking, **"Have you sorted through your loved one's belongings and, if so, what did you choose to do with them? What emotions did you struggle with most during this task?"** Allow each participant to answer then thank him/her for sharing before moving on to the next participant.

❏ **PAINFUL QUESTIONS & COMMENTS.** Mourners often face inflammatory questions and comments. Using the handout **PAINFUL QUESTIONS & COMMENTS,** guide the discussion by asking, **"Which questions or comments do you find most painful? What reply works best for you?"** Allow each participant to answer then thank him/her for sharing before moving on to the next participant.

5. **RESILIENCE RX**

❏ Remind participants of the importance of self-care as part of their griefwork. Going around the circle, invite participants to share a quick recap of how they did with their care plan by asking the following question, **"How did you do with your care plans?"**

❏ Invite them to review this session's handout and consider including it in their care plan.

6. **CONCLUSION**

Thank participants for coming and investing in their own well-being. Encourage them to:

❏ Read or review the session handouts
❏ Continue Bible work and journaling
❏ Add one activity to their self-care plan
❏ If desired, you can end with a poem, prayer, or group hug

COPING WITH BELONGINGS

Dealing with a deceased's belongings is one of the harder tasks for many. Because the items represent a direct link to our loved one, it can feel as though we're losing yet another piece of him/her. Deciding what to do with their clothes, toiletries, tools, mementos, keepsakes and other belongings—and when to do it—is an individual decision that's best guided by your heart.

WHAT TO KNOW

☑ **There is no right or wrong time.** The time frame for managing our deceased loved one's belongings and how exactly to go about it is unique to each of us. Some of us sort through, discard and/or donate our loved one's belongings immediately after the death. Others leave their loved one's belongings untouched for years.

☑ **Do it in your own time.** Some mourners feel pressured by family or friends to begin sorting through belongings fairly quickly. Yet, some of your supporters might not have the best of intentions, such as wanting something for themselves that they believe you no longer need. Don't allow external pressure to dictate your actions.

☑ **Do it at your own pace.** A deceased loved one often has years of accumulation that will take time to sort through. Unless you're under a hard timeline such as needing the space for something else or deciding to sell your home, there's no rule that says you can't take your time sorting through belongings. Go at your own speed.

☑ **Do it in your own space.** Some mourners find comfort when supporters help them. Others find comfort in tackling it in private. Do what feels best in that moment.

☑ **Don't make haste.** If in doubt about an item, keep it for now. You can always revisit what to do later but once you discard or donate an item, you can't undo it.

ANSWER THE FOLLOWING QUESTION

Without judging yourself, what have you done with your loved one's belongings? What emotions did you struggle with most during this task?

_____

_____

_____

_____

SESSION 3 | HANDOUT 14

QUESTIONS & COMMENTS

It's hard for people to see us in pain after loss, and it's a natural tendency for them to try to fix what appears broken. Although it's human nature to communicate using words, well intentioned statements can backfire in the emotional volatility of the moment.

Below are some of the comments that mourners can find inflammatory, and why (excerpted from *Grief Diaries: How to Help the Newly Bereaved,* 2016).

"How are you? Are you okay? This statement ignores the obvious and demands an answer.

"I understand how you feel." This statement tends to dismiss our intense emotions, and is especially inflammatory if the person saying it hasn't shared the same loss.

"Time heals all wounds." Time doesn't heal the pain. Instead, over the years the rawness softens and our coping skills become stronger.

"It will get better every day." Grief isn't a chronological process. One day can be good, but the next two might be very hard.

"Call if you need anything." The brain's stress hormones cloud logical thinking, and some of us fear being a burden.

"You need to stay strong." This often evokes guilt for crying.

You're so strong!" This often evokes confusion over why the mourner feels so weak.

"At least s/he isn't suffering." One's own suffering snuffs out all logic as to why we should be glad our loved one can't feel pain.

"God must have needed him/her." No matter how steadfast one is in his or her beliefs, a profound loss often triggers an examination of why our faith didn't protect our loved one.

"It's time to move on." The person making this statement implies that s/he knows what's best. Rushing through grief can hinder our progress.

"We all lose someone at some point," or "Loss is a part of life." While both are true, they lack compassion and dismiss one's right to move through the bereavement process.

ANSWER THE FOLLOWING QUESTION

What statement(s) do you find most inflammatory? How do they make you feel?

_____

_____

_____

GRIEF TYPES

Just as the grief journey is unique to each of us, there are also numerous types of grief. Below are some of the most common types mourners experience.

NORMAL GRIEF

This is what's considered a normal reaction to a loss event.

ANTICIPATORY GRIEF

Grieving an anticipated death before it occurs, common when a loved one is dying from a terminal illness.

TRAUMATIC GRIEF

Experiencing a sudden and unexpected loss; common when one has witnessed the actual death event.

COMPLICATED GRIEF

A grief reaction that occurs when one fails to work through their loss, continually experiencing extreme distress with no progress towards feeling better and no improvement in day-to-day functioning.

CUMULATIVE GRIEF

Experiencing a second loss while still grieving a prior loss. Also known as **grief overload**.

DELAYED GRIEF

Reacting much later to a death than is typical due to initial avoidance of the loss and emotional pain.

MASKED GRIEF

A reaction that impairs normal functioning without the individual recognizing that the behaviors are related to the loss. Symptoms are often masked as either physical symptoms or other maladaptive behaviors.

DISENFRANCHISED GRIEF

A rejection of one's mourning by their culture, family, social or work environment. The grief and suffering are disqualified by those around the mourner.

ABSENT GRIEF

Reacting to a major loss by blocking one's feelings as though it never happened. The individual shows no reaction at all and fails to give it importance in his or her life.

H15/GRIEF TYPES

ANSWER THE FOLLOWING QUESTION

Without judging yourself, what kind of grief do you believe you're experiencing?

_____

_____

_____

RESILIENCE RX TIP 3

SLEEP WELL

Losing a loved one creates upheaval that often leads to many sleepless nights. Juggling such emotional strains can cause serial tossing and turning, sleep disruption and insomnia. In turn, the ensuing sleep deprivation magnifies emotions and reduces our ability to cope with the upheaval.

CREATE A RITUAL

Creating a relaxing bedtime ritual gives your mind and body time to wind down. It sends a signal to your brain that bedtime is near, and trains it to go into quiet mode.

WHY IT MATTERS

Studies show that good sleep helps you cope better in times of stress. It can also improve your memory, lower blood pressure, help keep your immunity strong, and put you in a better mood.

Managing sleep disruption and insomnia by practicing good sleep hygiene, coupled with medical management when needed, can help restore a restful sleep pattern after loss, and lead to significant improvements in other distress symptoms (National Institutes of Health, 2008). If you continue struggling with sleepless nights after trying the tips below, consider seeing your doctor for further management.

SLEEP HYGIENE TIPS:

Try the following suggestions from the National Sleep Foundation to help you reestablish a restorative sleep pattern after losing someone you love.

- To help regulate your body's clock, stick to a sleep schedule of the same bedtime and wake time, even on weekends.

- Exercise early in the day. Vigorous exercise is best, but even light exercise is better than no exercise.

- A sleep environment between 60 and 67 degrees is ideal.

- If your partner snores, consider using a fan, earplugs, or white noise.

- Use comfortable pillows and bed linen.

- Consider moving bedroom furniture around, repainting the bedroom walls, and purchasing new bed linen.

- Avoid bright light in the evening to keep your circadian rhythm in check.

- Avoid caffeine, cigarettes, alcohol and heavy meals later in the day.

- Try wearing a weighted blanket across your feet and/or a sleep mask to help reduce stimuli and calm your mind.

R04/INSOMNIA

SESSION 3 | HANDOUT 17

BIBLE WORK

What does the Bible say about trauma?

But the pot he was shaping from the clay was marred in his hands; so the potter formed it into another pot, shaping it as seemed best to him.

JEREMIAH 18:4-6

SCRIPTURES TO EXPLORE

- ❑ ISAIAH 53:3-5
- ❑ JAMES 1:2
- ❑ II CORINTHIANS 4:6-7
- ❑ PSALM 34:18

There are two types of trauma we face. One type is the absence of nurturing we need from others, such as feeling cherished, loved, and validated. Another type is when bad things happen that never should have happened, such as premature death of a loved one, sexual and/or physical abuse.

No matter the trauma we experience, Jesus understands, for his whole life was full of suffering. He was born into poverty, persecuted, thought insane by his family, betrayed, deserted, arrested, tortured with a whip embedded with pieces of bone and metal, and executed.

It's been said that God shines best through broken vessels. Does trauma test our faith, or bring us closer to God? Does knowing that Jesus suffered much of his life bring us comfort when we, too, experience trauma?

WHAT DOES THE BIBLE SAY ABOUT TRAUMA?

Does the Bible's portrayal of trauma as a way to shine our light bring you comfort? If so, what scriptures do you find helpful?

ANSWER:

MY SCRIPTURES

Be the light
Ephesians 5:8

PRAYER

Dear God,

I feel broken in so many places, as though I have nothing left. My very soul feels as though it's been thrust into a fiery pit. Lord, help me to trust that you will forge something good from this, that my loved one's life and death will bring about goodness some way, some how.

Lord, please remind me that my light will shine once again, that this darkness isn't permanent. Until then, I ask that you help me to stay close to you, and give myself grace rather until my suffering eases. Thank you for hearing my cries, Lord.

In Jesus' name I pray, Amen.

A LETTER TO GOD

TODAY'S DATE: _____

Dear God,

I'm trusting the *Author* of my story

J29/A LETTER TO GOD

SESSION 4

FACING OUR FEARS

IC04/SESSION 4 INSTRUCTIONS

SESSION FORMAT

This session focuses on some of the ways grief creates fear. By verbalizing and facing these fears in the safety of the group, mourners feel less alone and can even learn from one another about how to cope with or manage what they fear most.

Following is this session's format:
1. Welcome and opening of session
2. Emotional check-in
3. Bible work check-in
4. Topic discussion
5. Review of self care
6. Conclusion

FACILITATION REMINDERS:

✓ Keep conversation moving. Protect conversation from being monopolized.

✓ Ensure every participant has an opportunity to answer the question. If the conversation jumps around the circle, be sure to circle back to those participants who haven't yet answered.

✓ If tension or disagreements flare during the discussion, reminder participants that this is a judgment-free zone and all perspectives are welcome.

✓ Stay neutral yet supportive.

LET'S BEGIN

1. **OPEN THE MEETING.**

Ask everyone to take a seat, open with the prayer on page 26 or one of your own, if desired, and then welcome them back to session #4. Thank them for investing in their future by being there.

FORMS & HANDOUTS

- ❑ **FORM**: My Participants
- ❑ **FORM**: Sign-in sheet
- ❑ HANDOUT 18: Coping with fear
- ❑ HANDOUT 19: Why grief robs our memory
- ❑ HANDOUT 20: Remembering the details
- ❑ HANDOUT 21: A letter to family & friends
- ❑ HANDOUT 22: Resilience Rx: Chromotherapy
- ❑ HANDOUT 23: Bible work

MATERIALS

- ❑ Workbooks
- ❑ Handouts
- ❑ Notebook & pen
- ❑ Nametags (if needed)
- ❑ Tissue
- ❑ Community resources
- ❑ Refreshments

2. EMOTIONAL CHECK-IN

❏ Going around the circle, ask participants one at a time the following question: **"If you could choose one word to describe your emotions today, what would you choose and why?"** Keep it short by limiting answers to about 30 to 60 seconds each. Thank each participant for sharing before moving on to the next participant.

3. BIBLE WORK

❏ Going around the circle, invite participants to share a quick recap of how they did with their bible work by asking the following question, **"How did you do with your Bible scriptures and journaling?"** Keep it short by limiting answers to 30 to 60 seconds each. Thank each participant for sharing before moving on to the next participant.

❏ Encourage participants to continue reading the Bible and journaling as part of their griefwork.

4. DISCUSSION: **Facing our fears**

❏ **FEAR.** In the aftermath of loss, many irrational fears can consume a mourner's thoughts. It's easy to become convinced that lightning can strike twice, and mourners often live in fear of that second strike. Using the handout **COPING WITH FEAR,** guide the discussion by asking, **"What fears have you struggled with most since your loss? How do you cope with them?"** Allow each participant to answer then thank him/her for sharing before moving on to the next participant.

❏ **FAMILY & FRIENDS.** Sometimes those in our support circle don't understand our journey. Using the handout **A LETTER FOR FAMILY & FRIENDS**, guide the discussion by asking, **"Which relationship has been impacted most by your loss? What do you want your family and friends to know about your journey?"** Allow each participant to answer before moving on to the next participant.

5. RESILIENCE RX

❏ Remind participants of the importance of self-care as part of their griefwork. Going around the circle, invite participants to share a quick recap of how they did with their care plan by asking the following question, **"How did you do with your care plans?"**

❏ Invite them to review this session's handout and consider including it in their care plan.

6. CONCLUSION

Thank participants for coming and investing in their own well-being. Encourage them to:
❏ Read or review the session handouts
❏ Continue Bible work and journaling
❏ Add one activity to their self-care plan
❏ If desired, you can end with a poem, prayer, or group hug

COPING WITH FEAR

In the aftermath of loss, fear can play a dominant role. Some fears are irrational, some not. It's easy to become convinced that lightning can strike twice, and our brains often live in fear of that second strike.

Those who have lost a loved one in a car accident might fear being in a car. Those who have lost a loved one to an illness might fear every cough or sneeze. A common fear for many is that we'll forget our loved one, as will the world. Below are fears commonly experienced by mourners (excerpted from *Grief Diaries: How to Help the Newly Bereaved,* 2016).

COMMON FEARS

1. **The future.** We fear what the future holds for us in the absence of our deceased loved one. We fear future holidays, future vacations, and future family members never knowing our loved one. We often fear making new memories without our loved one.

2. **Losing another loved one.** Because losing another loved one does sometimes happen, we fear it will happen to us a second time. The thought of facing the same wretched journey all over again strikes terror in our hearts.

3. **Failing to reach loved ones.** Because grief heightens our fear of losing another loved one, when we fail to reach those we love on the phone or the computer, anxiety can build rather quickly triggering a wave of panic.

4. **Traveling.** Whether we've lost a loved one in a crash or not, traveling can exacerbate the fear of losing another loved one in a car, plane, bus, boat, bike or some other means of transportation.

5. **Being alone or growing old alone.** Widows and widowers often fear never being loved again.

6. **Lifetime repercussions for our loved ones.** Sometimes we fear that those we love feel just as sad as we do, and it's instinct to want to protect them from such pain. We fear they won't recover from the loss, or that the grief will force them down the wrong path.

7. **Feeling sad forever.** Grief sadness can feel so overwhelming that we fear it will never evaporate. We fear living a joyless life forever.

8. **Falling apart or feeling "crazy" forever.** We fear giving in and allowing ourselves to do the griefwork for fear we'll never survive the pain.

9. **Forgetting details about our loved one.** We fear we'll forget the little things such as the smell of their hair, the sound of their voice, their laughter, their little mannerisms, or what their hug feels like.

10. **Our loved one being forgotten.** We fear our deceased loved one will be forgotten by others, leaving us to carry the grief burden alone.

11. **Someone who looks like our love one.** When we see someone who resembles our loved one, it steals our breath and is like a kick in the stomach. It's hard to hold the tears back.

12. **The holidays.** We fear seeing the empty chair and family traditions that will never feel the same.

13. **Dying.** When we lose a loved one, we often fear dying ourselves. If we die too soon, what happens to those we care for? Who will take care of them? Who will wipe their tears?

14. **Returning to work.** We often fear what coworkers and colleagues will think. Will they feel uncomfortable around us? Will they ignore our loss and pretend nothing happened? Will they ask too many questions? Will I make it through the day without being triggered?

TIPS FOR COPING

1. **Acknowledge the fear.** Facing fear head-on can help to eliminate some of its power.

2. **Expect irrational fears.** This is normal, as grief exacerbates or heightens many of our fears.

3. **Take time to understand.** A fear can be severe. Take time to understand the root of the fear (rejection, failure, etc.) without judgment.

4. **Create a plan.** Proactive planning is empowering. Identify what you fear most and create a plan so you feel more in control.

5. **Patience is key.** Find a safe outlet to share and vent your fears. Externalizing them in a safe environment will eventually allow you to process your fears and work through them.

ANSWER THE FOLLOWING QUESTION

What fears have you struggled with most since your loss?

H18/COPING WITH FEAR

WHY GRIEF ROBS OUR MEMORY

Memory is something I used to take for granted, at least up until 2009, when my 15-year-old daughter Aly died in a car accident.

Nobody told me I would lose my memory after losing a child. It was so bad I often worried about early onset Alzheimer's.

You too?

The good news is that we're not alone.

The better news is that there's an explanation, and it's not because we're going crazy.

It turns out that during trauma such as the death of a loved one, the fear region of our brain known as the amygdala triggers a flood of stress hormones, mainly cortisol, adrenaline, and norepinephrine. Largely responsible for the body's natural flight-fight-freeze-fawn response, these hormones are designed to protect us in a life-threatening situation by triggering a burst of energy.

The downside is that these same stress hormones anesthetize the frontal cortex of the brain where critical thinking and problem solving skills are located.

Memory is impacted, time gets distorted, and events come back like a strobe light rather than a story.

So, if nobody told you that memory loss, tunnel vision and time distortion are normal responses to emotional trauma, rest assured it's common.

I promise.

Symptoms are especially pronounced after an unexpected, traumatic loss.

Yes, I know—memory loss due to grief is still very embarrassing. Especially to our kids.

Next time your kids give you the stink eye for asking the same question you did fifteen minutes ago, bore them with the above explanation. With luck, they'll never question your sanity again.

At least not out loud.

LYNDA CHELDELIN FELL
H19/WHY GRIEF ROBS OUR MEMORY

REMEMBERING THE DETAILS

Many mourners fear forgetting the little details that made their loved one so special. Use the prompts below to document details about your loved one that offers a snapshot of who s/he was, and what you want future generations of your family to know about your loved one. If you don't recall every detail, that's okay. Just record what you remember.

MY LOVED ONE'S NAME: _____

DATE OF DEATH: _____   AGE AT TIME OF DEATH: _____

CAUSE OF DEATH: _____

MY LOVED ONE'S EYE COLOR: _____

MY LOVED ONE'S NATURAL HAIR COLOR: _____

MY LOVED ONE'S HAIR COLOR AT TIME OF DEATH: _____

MY LOVED ONE'S HEIGHT: _____   MY LOVED ONE'S WEIGHT: _____

MY LOVED ONE'S SHIRT SIZE: _____   MY LOVED ONE'S SHOE SIZE: _____

MY LOVED ONE'S CLOTHING STYLE: _____

_____

MY LOVED ONE'S BODY ART INCLUDED: _____

_____

MY LOVED ONE HAD A _____

_____

_____

_____

Example: Good heart, gentle soul, witty personality

MY LOVED ONE MADE A GOOD

Example: Good lasagna, potato salad, scrapbook, quilt

MY LOVED ONE WAS A GOOD

Example: Friend, gardener, knitter, painter, poem writer, helper, leader

PEOPLE WOULD SAY MY LOVED ONE WAS

Example: Funny, kind, smart, gentle, generous, humble, creative

MY LOVED ONE'S TALENTS INCLUDED

Example: Finding things, good memory, witty comments, applying makeup, keeping room tidy, etc.

MY LOVED ONE ENJOYED:

_____

_____

_____

Example: Taking baths, drinking cocoa before bed, wearing cushy socks, lighting a fragrant candle, going to the beach, etc.

MY LOVED ONE'S FAVORITE BOOK OR BOOK GENRE:

_____

_____

_____

Example: Harry Potter series, romance, science fiction, home decorating

MY LOVED ONE'S FAVORITE SCENT OR FRAGRANCE:

_____

_____

Example: Citrus, sugar cookies, seashore, Victoria Secret perfume, Hugo Boss cologne, fresh-cut grass

MY LOVED ONE'S FAVORITE SONG(S) OR BAND(S):

_____

_____

_____

_____

MY LOVED ONE'S FAVORITE HOBBIES

Example: Beading, woodworking, magic tricks, bike riding, scrapbooking, rock collecting, fishing, etc.

MY LOVED ONE'S FAVORITE GAMES

Example: Monopoly, Hide 'n Seek, Go Fish, Scrabble, Pokémon, video games, etc.

MY LOVED ONE'S FAVORITE STORES

Example: Dollar Store, the mall, Victoria Secret, Cabela's, Wal-Mart, Target, Nordstroms

MY LOVED ONE'S FAVORITE VACATION SPOT OR TRIP

MY LOVED ONE WAS MOST LIKE ME IN THESE WAYS:

_____

_____

_____

MY LOVED ONE WAS DIFFERENT FROM ME IN THESE WAYS:

_____

_____

_____

_____

MY LOVED ONE MADE A DIFFERENCE IN THE WORLD BECAUSE:

_____

_____

_____

_____

_____

_____

THINGS I WANT FUTURE GENERATIONS OF MY FAMILY TO KNOW ABOUT MY LOVED ONE:

_____

_____

_____

_____

_____

_____

_____

_____

A LETTER TO FAMILY & FRIENDS

Dear loved ones,

Loss has far-reaching effects in life, and can have a lasting impact on relationships. Sometimes our deep fondness for those we care about can be frayed and even fractured by lack of understanding. Losing a loved one doesn't come with instructions, leaving many people confused about what to expect. Below is a list of things I want you to know about my grief journey.

Thank you for taking the time to read this.

WHAT I WANT YOU TO KNOW

1. **You can't fix grief.** It's natural to want to fix things that appear broken, but grief is beyond your repair. Don't feel guilty about it. It's also helpful to remember that if a simple statement or gesture could fix it, I would have done it by now.

2. **Crying is normal.** Crying is a healthy response to emotional pain. Suppressed grief leads to complications. As talking and crying go hand in hand, the gift of listening without judgment can help.

3. **Grief is predictably unpredictable.** My emotions will be unpredictable for a few years; so will my reactions. My reactions will mirror the emotions I'm feeling in that moment. Just hold the space as I learn to work through it myself.

4. **Emotional overloads can lead to reactive meltdowns.** Please be patient with me. A good night's sleep or nap can help me cope better the next day. I'll do my best to get good rest.

5. **Grief is exhausting.** Exhaustion makes us all crabby. Avoid overloading me with distractions, and help me learn to reduce stressors.

6. **Don't take it personally.** Sometimes my emotional distress causes me to react in less than graceful ways. Already overwhelmed by our feelings, small issues can quickly feel insurmountable. I don't mean to take it out on you. Really, I don't.

7. **Don't be afraid.** It's okay to talk about it, my wound is already open. Also, it's okay for me to not be okay as I do the griefwork needed to process my loss.

8. **Your cues count.** Expect me to give you guarded answers if your physical cues give away your hesitancy or discomfort.

9. **I don't have all the answers either.** Grief doesn't come with an instruction manual. I wish it did.

10. **Full of surprises.** Because I'm feeling emotionally raw, I might lose my filters sometimes. Prepare for offhanded comments or responses, and trust that eventually I'll regain my footing.

11. **Have compassion.** When you point out that I'm repeating myself or I can't remember details, it makes me feel worse. Help me to remember important details or tasks.

12. **Grief is more than just an emotional wound.** Grief is a severe injury to one's heart and soul. For this reason, it is helpful to think of me as a patient in the intensive care unit of Grief United Hospital. Treat me as you would any other hospital patient: with tender loving care, compassion and kindness.

13. **Grief is a long rollercoaster ride.** It is often compared to a rollercoaster because it contains many emotional twists and blind turns at varying speeds. It is very unpredictable and can feel quite scary. And, as much as I try, I simply cannot control the speed, put the brakes on, nor can I predict the twists and turns. Neither can you.

14. **Don't judge or dispute my progress.** This implies that you're domineering and lack compassion. If you insist you know better, I might respond with resentment that can severely damage our relationship.

15. **Your timeline isn't my timeline.** The grief process and timeline are unique to every individual, and I might grieve in subtle ways for the rest of my life. Applying your timeline to my journey can lead to disappointment.

16. **Isolation is common.** Like a wounded animal in the wild, I'll sometimes want to hibernate away from social interaction. If it is safe to leave me alone, then please honor my wishes.

17. **Ignoring grief is dangerous.** My grief won't go away any faster when you ignore it, and doing so can actually prolong it. Ignoring grief can also cause further complications such as health issues and suicidal ideation. Please don't ignore my griefwork. It's important to my future.

18. **There are many grief stages.** In 1969, Dr. Elisabeth Kübler-Ross theorized that there are five stages of grief experienced by the terminally ill, not the loved ones left behind. The truth is that grief is messy, and my journey isn't always linear. Just help me take it one day at a time.

HOW WE THINK GRIEF WORKS

HOW GRIEF ACTUALLY WORKS

19. **Grief creates fear.** Sometimes my fears might seem irrational yet I can't help myself. Simple and loving reassurance really helps. So does engaging me in conversation.

20. **Eventually I will find my way.** Learning to live without my loved one is a long, hard journey. Eventually, the rawness will soften and my coping skill will strengthen. I just need you to walk beside me until I can feel joy again.

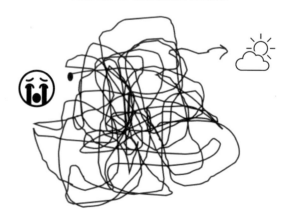

RESILIENCE RX TIP 4

CHROMOTHERAPY

Colors are all around us, and they aren't meaningless. They play a role in how we feel, and can influence our emotions and how we react.

Chromotherapy is an ancient practice, yet researchers are just now beginning to understand how it works as a healing modality as they study how colors affect our brain and emotions.

HELPFUL TIP

When you need to relax, grab a coloring book or color the following pages. Use crayons, colored pencils, gel pens or felt pens to color each picture using whatever colors match your emotions in that moment.

WHY IT MATTERS

What we know about chromotherapy is that it calms the amygdala, the fear center of the brain. It also takes us outside the thinking part of our brain. Certain colors can invigorate a depressed mood or soothe an agitated mind, lower blood pressure, and relax breathing.

BENEFITS OF ADULT COLORING

Most of us loved coloring as a child. Its popularity as an activity for grownups has exploded, and for good reason. The repetitive hand motions used in coloring induces a meditative state. Focusing on the simple act of coloring gives our brain a respite from pain. It unplugs it from negativity and plugs it into positivity by focusing on the present rather than our worries.

The beauty of coloring is that it can be done by anyone regardless of creative talent, and you can take it with you wherever you go. Pick colors that reflect your current mood to help safely externalize your feelings.

MORE WAYS TO USE COLOR TO TRIGGER POSITIVE HORMONES:

- Paint a color-by-number picture
- Color your bath water
- Plug in a colored nightlight
- Hang a colored glass prism
- Paint the walls of your bedroom or office

- Add colorful home décor
- Use colored bulbs in your lamps
- Enjoy a colorwash YouTube video
- Download a color therapy app
- Enjoy a chromotherapy sauna

©JOANNE FINK·WWW.ZENSPIRATIONS.COM

Copyright © 2017 Color Your Soul Whole

©JOANNE FINK·WWW.ZENSPIRATIONS.COM

SESSION 4 | HANDOUT 23

BIBLE WORK

What does the Bible say about fear?

I sought the Lord, and he answered me and delivered me from all my fears.

PSALM 34:4

SCRIPTURES TO EXPLORE

- ☐ ISAIAH 41:10
- ☐ 1 JOHN 4:18
- ☐ JOSHUA 1:9
- ☐ SECOND TIMOTHY 1:7

The Bible is filled with stories of people who overcame their fears with the strength of God. The term "fear not" is stated in the Bible over 300 times.

Fear has the potential to paralyze us. Yet, while the Bible instructs us to fight against the strongholds of fear, some struggle with this concept. Since God didn't protect their loved one from death, will lightning strike twice?

In **Psalm 34:4**, King David sought the Lord and He answered, delivering King David of his fears. How did King David hand it over? Did he trust God, and let him have full control?

Through His Word, God tells us there is nothing to fear, yet it's human nature to want to control things we fear, instead of trusting God. Loss of a loved one creates very real fears for many. In **John 16:33**, Jesus tells us that we will have tribulations in the world but to be of good cheer since he has overcome the world.

So then, what do we fear? Is the spirit of fear an attack from the devil when we're at our weakest? If so, why doesn't God protect us from the devil's assault? Does fear test our faith, or bring us closer to God?

MY SCRIPTURES

WHAT DOES THE BIBLE SAY ABOUT FEAR?

Does the Bible's portrayal of fear bring comfort? If so, what scriptures do you find helpful?

ANSWER:

iCare

Be the light
Ephesians 5:8

PRAYER

Dear God,

Fear of many things has taken hold of my heart. I fear the future without my loved one. I fear losing another loved one. I fear I will never feel joy again. I fear I won't feel your comfort during my season of grief.

Lord, I ask you to ease the fear in my heart, and to give me strength to bear my sadness. I thank you for holding such heavy burdens for me, and ask you to help me give them all to you to carry.

In Jesus' name I pray, Amen.

A LETTER TO GOD

TODAY'S DATE: _____

Dear God,

I'm trusting the *Author* of my story

SESSION 5

DATES & HOLIDAYS

IC05/SESSION 5 INSTRUCTIONS

SESSION FORMAT

This session focuses on how we cope with calendar dates and holidays that are most painful. By verbalizing and sharing how we cope in the safety of the group, mourners feel less alone and can even learn from one another about how to cope with or manage predictably painful times.

Following is this session's format:

1. Welcome and opening of session
2. Emotional check-in
3. Bible work check-in
4. Topic discussion
5. Review of self care
6. Conclusion

FACILITATION REMINDERS:

✓ Keep conversation moving. Protect conversation from being monopolized.

✓ Ensure every participant has an opportunity to answer the question. If the conversation jumps around the circle, be sure to circle back to those participants who haven't yet answered.

✓ If tension or disagreements flare during the discussion, reminder participants that this is a judgment-free zone and all perspectives are welcome.

✓ Stay neutral yet supportive.

LET'S BEGIN

1. **OPEN THE MEETING.**

   ❑ Ask everyone to take a seat and then open with the prayer on page 26 or one of your own, if desired, and welcome them back to session #5. Thank them for investing in their future by being there.

FORMS & HANDOUTS

❑ **FORM**: My Participants
❑ **FORM**: Sign-in sheet
❑ **HANDOUT 24**: Coping with painful dates
❑ **HANDOUT 25**: Coping with holidays
❑ **HANDOUT 26**: Tips for supporters
❑ **HANDOUT 27**: 12 Nights of Kindness
❑ **HANDOUT 28**: Resilience Rx: Music therapy
❑ **HANDOUT 29**: Bible work

MATERIALS

❑ Workbooks
❑ Handouts
❑ Notebook & pen
❑ Nametags (if needed)
❑ Tissue
❑ Community resources
❑ Refreshments

2. **EMOTIONAL CHECK-IN**

 ❏ Going around the circle, ask participants one at a time the following question: **"If you could choose one word to describe your emotions today, what would you choose and why?"** Keep it short by limiting answers to about 30 to 60 seconds each. Thank each participant for sharing before moving on to the next participant.

3. **BIBLE WORK**

 ❏ Going around the circle, invite participants to share a quick recap of how they did with their bible work by asking the following question, **"How did you do with your Bible scriptures and journaling?"** Keep it short by limiting answers to about 30 to 60 seconds each. Thank each participant for sharing before moving on to the next participant.

 ❏ Encourage participants to continue reading the Bible and journaling as part of their griefwork.

4. **DISCUSSION: Coping with painful dates and holidays**

 ❏ **DATES.** In the aftermath of loss, many mourners find certain cyclical dates to be extra painful and triggering, such as birthdays and anniversaries. Using the handout **COPING WITH PAINFUL DATES,** guide the discussion by asking, **"What days are extra painful for you, and how do you cope?"** Allow each participant to answer then thank him/her for sharing before moving on to the next participant.

 ❏ **HOLIDAYS.** Because of traditions, certain holidays can be especially triggering for mourners. Using the handout **COPING WITH HOLIDAYS,** guide the discussion by asking, **"Which holiday is most painful for you? Do you prefer to stick with family traditions, or try something different?"** Allow each participant to answer then thank him/her for sharing before moving on to the next participant.

5. **RESILIENCE RX**

 ❏ Remind participants of the importance of self-care as part of their griefwork. Going around the circle, invite participants to share a quick recap of how they did with their care plan by asking the following question, **"How did you do with your care plans?"**

 ❏ Invite them to review this session's handout and consider including it in their care plan.

6. **CONCLUSION**

Thank participants for coming and investing in their own well-being. Encourage them to:

 ❏ Read or review the session handouts
 ❏ Continue Bible work and journaling
 ❏ Add one activity to their self-care plan
 ❏ If desired, you can end with a poem, prayer, or group hug

COPING WITH PAINFUL DATES

Grief is a profound, complex injury that is tricky to handle because it bares no physical wounds. And it's also predictably unpredictable. But one thing is absolute: certain calendar dates can be triggering, heightening our emotional volatility. Although these calendar dates come around like clockwork, most of these dates may remain sensitive for the rest of our life. It is something we eventually learn to cope with. Our loved one's birthday, the anniversary of their death, Mother's Day, Father's Day, other anniversaries like wedding anniversaries, are predictably the worst.

WHAT TO KNOW

1. **Some calendar dates may always remain emotionally charged.**

   - The loved one's birthday
   - The anniversary of his/her death
   - Mother's Day
   - Father's Day
   - The loved one's favorite holiday(s)
   - Most family-oriented holidays

2. **The rollercoaster returns.** Be aware of the emotional sensitivity you're likely to witness around these dates.

3. **Go at your own pace.** What felt good last year might not feel good this year.

4. **Plan for triggers.** Be cognizant of your triggers around these dates and take steps to plan for them.

5. **Do not expect others to understand.** Certain dates may remain painful for a long time, and others around you may be unaware that such dates remain triggering. Consider educating them about triggers.

6. **Just be.** Accept that there is simply nothing you can do to stop certain dates from being painful. Be kind to yourself and give yourself grace around these times.

ANSWER THE FOLLOWING QUESTION

What calendar dates do you find most painful?

WAYS TO COPE

Acknowledge the dates. Validate and acknowledge to your support circle that these dates are extra sensitive. This will encourage family and friends to extend compassion.

Solitude is normal. If you feel like spending the day in quiet solitude, ask family and friends not to barrage you with questions as to whether you are okay. Remind them that you are not okay, but you'll weather it.

Invite others to do something meaningful. Some mourners might welcome a distraction. If you find that helpful, invite others to join you in doing something meaningful that day.

Enjoy. Celebrate your loved one by visiting their favorite restaurant and enjoying their favorite dinner or dessert.

Take part. Participate in an activity your loved one enjoyed as a way to honor them.

Visit the cemetery. Leave flowers or a remembrance token at your loved one's gravesite for others to enjoy when they visit.

Celebrate. Write notes on balloons and release them.

Adorn a tree. Tie a ribbon around a neighborhood tree in your loved one's favorite color.

Pay it forward. Pay it forward in memory of your loved one. A random act of kindness can trigger endorphins to offset the sadness.

Cook. Prepare your loved one's favorite meal and invite others to enjoy it with you.

Watch a movie. Watch your loved one's favorite movie.

Wear it. Wear clothes in your loved one's favorite color.

Send it. Send flowers or a gift basket in memory of your loved one to someone in need.

Donate it. Consider distributing Blessing Bags to the homeless or a women's shelter. Compile toiletries from the local dollar store into decorative bags and give them to those in need. This is a gentle reminder that we aren't alone in our struggles, and the gift of giving can trigger endorphins to offset the sadness.

ANSWER THE FOLLOWING QUESTION

What are some strategies you use to help you cope with painful calendar dates?

SESSION 5 | HANDOUT 25

COPING WITH HOLIDAYS

Whether it be the holiday season, Valentine's Day, or Fourth of July, facing any major holiday after losing our loved one—especially our loved one's favorite holiday—is a nostalgic reminder of merrier times and can hark the herald of unending tears.

Allow yourself to try a handful of these tips to guide you through the emotional kaleidoscope. Above all, do what feels best to your heart, and self-gift with big doses of kindness and compassion.

HELPFUL TIPS

Stick with a routine. A familiar routine offers a sense of reassurance that at least one thing in life hasn't changed, and the familiarity can help us feel grounded. But if it feels too painful, then do what feels best to you in that moment.

Avoid packing the schedule. Grieving is emotionally exhausting; plenty of rest will help minimize raw nerves.

Cut yourself some slack, not your finger. Grieving is naturally distracting. Even the smallest kitchen disaster can quickly deplete coping skills. Buy store-bought when possible.

Skip the chaos. Turn off the computer, light a fragrant candle, grab a soft blanket, and binge-watch a good comedy. Take time to create peaceful surroundings to soothe your nerves.

Treat your senses to TLC. Each day acknowledge 5 things you can see, 4 things you can feel, 3 things you can hear, 2 things you can smell, and 1 thing you can taste.

When the mood strikes. Give yourself permission to feel joy without guilt. The heart can hold both and it's good for the spirit.

Honor the past. Find a way to include your loved one's memory. Hang their stocking and fill it with cat toys or dog treats for the family pet, or pay it forward in your loved one's name.

Volunteer. Do something in the community that lifts your spirits. It induces a "helper's high" that's good for both the brain and the heart. It also reminds us we're not alone in our struggles.

Seek support. Surround yourself with others who speak your loss language and fully understand how hard the holidays can be.

Cry. Give in to the tears. There is no shortage of raw emotions over the holidays, and a good cry can be cleansing and help release emotional buildup.

REMEMBER

The heart can hold joy the same time as sorrow. Allow yourself respites from the sadness and enjoy holiday festivities as much as you can without guilt.

HOLIDAY TIPS FOR SUPPORTERS

Dear family and friends,

Holidays are a cherished time of year for everyone. Because many holidays are steeped in tradition, memories of past holidays magnify emotions of both my loss and the finality that my loved one will never be part of family photos and other traditions ever again.

Until my rawness softens, below is a list of ways you can support me through painful holidays.

HOW YOU CAN HELP

- **Recognize that you can't fix my sorrow.** Trust that I'm working hard at processing my grief. I just ask that you hold the space for me to do it myself.

- **Honor my choice for how I wish to cope** with the holidays, even if you don't agree. Trust my instinct that I know what's best for me.

- **Do not avoid me.** If I ask to be left alone, honor my wish if it's safe to do so. Otherwise, include me in the festivities and treat me like any other guest: with kindness.

- **Resist the urge to fill my calendar** with festivities as a way to cheer or distract me. Just like all healing, grieving is exhausting and I may not have the energy to keep up.

- **Don't let my sorrow deplete your own joy.** Give yourself permission to enjoy all the festivities without guilt.

- **Expect me to have cranky moments.** It's human nature for pain to overload one's emotions. Further, because the holiday season is a busy time and grief is naturally exhausting, my emotional threshold for holiday overload is much lower. If you are having difficulty finding compassion during one of my cranky moments, go do something fun to recharge your battery.

- **Invite me to help you volunteer in the community.** Serving others less fortunate is a wonderful reminder that I'm not alone in my struggles.

- **Help me honor my loved one** during the holidays. We can pay it forward in my loved one's memory. We can leave a bouquet of balloons in my loved one's favorite color in a public spot for a stranger to find while we both watch discreetly. Or we can donate to a cause that was close to my loved one's heart.

- **If I get caught up in the merriment, celebrate with me** but be patient if the moment doesn't last long. With time, moments of joy will grow as the rawness softens.

As always, thank you for taking the time to read this.

H26/HOLIAY TIPS FOR SUPPORTERS

12 NIGHTS OF KINDNESS

Have you heard of the 12 Nights of Christmas?

Also known as Secret Santa, I came across this idea years before I experienced my own loss. Modeled after the *12 days of Christmas*, beginning on December 13 and ending on Christmas Eve, every evening a family anonymously drops a poem with a corresponding treat on the porch of a neighbor in need. On Christmas Eve, the sneaking family reveals their identity. The whole idea is to teach kids that giving is just as fun as receiving.

Inspired by the idea of helping my kids learn the joys of giving at their young age, that December we adopted the tradition as our own.

Our oldest daughter was at college and our teenage son was a busy highschooler, so that left our two youngest kids. As I explained what we were embarking on and why, they were thrilled with the idea of playing a secret Santa.

Our 10-year-old daughter Aly much preferred to be an elf, given that she was female and Santa was, well, male. But, if her 8-year-old brother Shaun was Santa—an elf's superior—that wouldn't do either. To keep the peace, they both became elves instead of Santas.

As a family of six with one in college, we were on a budget. Armed with a shopping list, my first stop was our local dollar store. Thankfully, everything we needed was there.

Taking home supplies, we got to work printing the poems and preparing the treats while the kids giggled at the notion of twelve nights of mischief over the holidays.

It was already December, and the first night was fast approaching. Fairly new to the neighborhood, we discussed who should be the recipient. I had heard that Tom, a neighbor a few blocks over, had recently lost his wife to cancer and was now a widower.

I couldn't imagine what the holidays must be like for Tom and their two kids. To my mind, it was clear that their home could use small doses of nightly cheer. We all agreed, and the matter was settled.

On the evening of December 13, my two little elves giggled nervously as we bundled up and headed out into the night. Sneaking through the quiet snow-filled lanes of our neighborhood was as magical for the kids as it was for me; I treasured our memories in the making.

We successfully delivered the first poem and, per the instructions, a partridge ornament. Upon returning home, we thawed our hands around a mug of hot cocoa, and warmed our hearts around the notion that our nightly surprises might bring cheer to Tom's family.

The next eleven nights flew by and soon it was Christmas Eve—the day when we had to reveal our identity.

I woke up that morning feeling nervous. We had never actually met Tom, and I was worried that perhaps our nightly gifts had been a bit too much for the family's fragile emotions. But there was no backing down; we had to finish.

That afternoon, as per the instructions, we arranged 12 homemade cookies on a small paper plate, covered it with red cellophane, taped the final poem to the top, and off to Tom's we went, this time in broad daylight. But, were Tom and his kids even home? We didn't know but would soon find out.

With treats in hand, we gathered on Tom's front porch, and I rang the doorbell.

When Tom opened the door, we nervously started singing:

> *We wish you a merry Christmas*
> *We wish you a merry Christmas*
> *We wish you a merry Christmas,*
> *and a happy new year!*

To my horror, I ended up singing alone—my two elves stood glued to the porch with mouths frozen shut. Because I'm tone deaf, I quickly decided that one verse was more than enough for this poor family. As soon as I quit singing, I realized that Tom and his two kids had tears in their eyes!

Oh dear. Was my voice that bad, or was our entire mission just a big flop?

I decided the best way to handle this was to introduce ourselves and explain we were the little elves responsible for the nightly treats, and then hastily leave the poor family alone. After all, it was Christmas Eve and we were strangers intruding on their fragile emotions.

But I soon discovered I had nothing to fear at all—Tom and his kids were crying because of how much they loved the gifts, and now it was coming to an end!

It turns out that Tom and his kids not only enjoyed the element of surprise, but the nightly anticipation was a wonderful respite from the constant sadness.

Mission accomplished!

That first year proved a wonderful experience and we continued the tradition, choosing a different neighbor each year. That is, until our own tragedy struck.

In 2009, Aly, now 15, died in a car crash while coming home from a swim meet. Caught in my own fog of grief, I had no joy to share and no energy to carry on the family fun with Shaun, who was now 13.

With broken hearts, our beloved tradition came to an unexpected end. Or so I thought.

In the years since losing Aly, in fits and starts our family learned to laugh and feel joy again but I've never forgotten how bleak those first holidays felt. I've also learned that helping others helped my own heart to heal.

When our grandson turned 9—the perfect age to become an elf—I reinstated the old family tradition. Just as it had in years past, it offered both giver and receiver a nightly dose of good cheer, and once again enriched our holiday in magical ways.

In the years since, I've never forgotten Tom. Having faced loss since then ourselves, I now fully understand how the holidays can feel quite bleak, and how a little kindness can go a long way.

Overall, the nightly trips to an unsuspecting porch are more than just fun. People of all ages can be agents of kindness, and giving others the priceless gift of cheer anytime of year is a gift of joy we give ourselves. Happy holidays!

LYNDA CHELDELIN FELL
VISIT WWW.LYNDAFELL.COM FOR INSTRUCTIONS

RESILIENCE RX TIP 5

MUSIC THERAPY

Music therapy is an evidence-based treatment that uses music to help improve coping, reduce stress, and assist with self reflection and expression of thoughts and emotions. Formal music therapy was defined and first used by the U.S. War Department in 1945 to help military service members recovering in Army hospitals.

BENEFITS

✓ Helps to release bottled emotions

✓ Stimulates the brain

✓ Lowers blood pressure

✓ Relaxes the body by reducing muscle tension

✓ Stimulates tapping and body movements

✓ Distracts from pain

✓ Provides an increased sense of control

✓ Decreases anxiety, fatigue and depression

HOW TO ENGAGE

Music is a powerful way to soothe the heart, invoke memories, and honor our loved ones. Regardless of skill or talent, one can engage in music therapy through listening to songs that match or uplift your mood, singing out loud, playing an instrument, and/or composing music.

SONGS TO TRY

- Wind Beneath My Wings, by Bette Midler

- Angels, by Robbie Williams

- Something You Get Through, by Willie Nelson

- I'll Be Missing You, by Puff Daddy

- Somewhere Over the Rainbow, by Harold Arlen & Yip Harburg

- Tears in Heaven, by Eric Clapton

- Unforgettable, by Natalie Cole

- Candle in the Wind, by Elton John

- To Where You Are, by Josh Groban

- Keep Me in Your Heart, by Warren Zevon

- Calling All Angels, by Train

- Angel, by Sarah McLachlan

- Knockin' on Heaven's Door, by Bob Dylan

- Bridge Over Troubled Water, by Simon & Garfunkel

- See You Again, by Carrie Underwood

- I Will Always Love you, by Whitney Houston

- Amazing Grace, Christian hymn by John Newton

- Unchained Melody, by The Righteous Brothers

- Yesterday, by The Beatles

SESSION 5 | HANDOUT 29

BIBLE WORK

What does the Bible say about mourning through the holidays?

For to us a child is born, to us a son is given;
and the government shall be upon his shoulder,
and his name shall be called Wonderful Counselor,
Mighty God, Everlasting Father, Prince of Peace.

ISAIAH 9:6-7

SCRIPTURES TO EXPLORE

- ❏ **PHILIPPIANS 4:7**
- ❏ **2 CORINTHIANS 13:11**
- ❏ **COLOSSIANS 2:1-3:25**

The holidays, specifically Christmas and Easter, are a time of great joy as we honor Jesus, both his birth and his ascension to heaven. Yet as joyful as they are, facing the holidays after losing a loved one is a nostalgic reminder of merrier times and can hark the herald of unending tears. How do we manage this extra layer of grief during times of great joy for other Christians?

In **Isaiah 7:14-15**, we're told that Mary the virgin shall conceive and bear a son, and call him Immanuel. Upon his birth, surely Mary was rejoicing the newborn's life in a wooden cradle not knowing his demise would take place on a wooden cross. Yet, we can only imagine the great grief she felt as she witnessed her son's torturous death.

In **2 Corinthians 13:11**, we are told to rejoice, comfort one another, and live in peace, for God's peace and love shall be with us. Yet, the pain of grief can feel crushing even to the most faithful. Do we trust in God only when we feel joyful? Can God's Word bring peace to our hearts through the holidays? How do we hold on to God's hands like Mary did, instead of hanging by a thread?

WHAT DOES THE BIBLE SAY ABOUT MOURNING THROUGH THE HOLIDAYS?

Do Christian holidays comfort or sadden you, or both? What scriptures do you find helpful?

ANSWER:

MY SCRIPTURES

Be the light
Ephesians 5:8

PRAYER

Dear God,

I used to rejoice in holidays, especially Christian holidays, now they cause an extra layer of sadness because my loved one isn't here to share them with. I feel the pain of their absence more than ever.

Lord, I thank you for the joy the holidays bring. I know our hearts can hold joy the same time as sorrow so, Lord, I humbly ask you to help me open my heart to moments of joy as a respite from the constant sorrow. Thank you for hearing my cries, Lord, and giving me strength to endure.

In Jesus' name I pray, Amen.

A LETTER TO GOD

TODAY'S DATE: _____

Dear God,

_____

_____

_____

_____

_____

_____

_____

_____

_____

_____

_____

_____

_____

_____

_____

_____

I'm trusting the *Author* of my story

SESSION 6

LIFE, DEATH & FAITH

IC06/SESSION 6 INSTRUCTIONS

SESSION FORMAT

This session focuses on exploring what our personal belief is about the purpose of life and what role faith plays in our journey. By verbalizing and sharing what we believe in the safety of this group, mourners learn from one another.

Following is this session's format:
1. Welcome and opening of session
2. Emotional check-in
3. Bible work check-in
4. Topic discussion
5. Review of self care
6. Conclusion

FACILITATION REMINDERS:

✓ Keep conversation moving. Protect conversation from being monopolized.

✓ Ensure every participant has an opportunity to answer the question. If the conversation jumps around the circle, be sure to circle back to those participants who haven't yet answered.

✓ If tension or disagreements flare during the discussion, reminder participants that this is a judgment-free zone and all perspectives are welcome.

✓ Stay neutral yet supportive.

LET'S BEGIN

1. **OPEN THE MEETING.**

   ❑ Ask everyone to take a seat, open with the prayer on page 26 or one of your own, if desired, and then welcome them back to session #6. Thank them for investing in their future by being there.

FORMS & HANDOUTS

❑ **FORM**: My Participants
❑ **FORM**: Sign-in sheet
❑ HANDOUT 30: What do I believe?
❑ HANDOUT 31: The purpose of life
❑ HANDOUT 32: Faith & Death
❑ HANDOUT 33: God's script
❑ HANDOUT 34: Resilience Rx: Dance/movement therapy
❑ HANDOUT 35: Bible work

MATERIALS

❑ Workbooks
❑ Handouts
❑ Notebook & pen
❑ Nametags (if needed)
❑ Tissue
❑ Community resources
❑ Refreshments

2. **EMOTIONAL CHECK-IN**

❑ Going around the circle, ask participants one at a time the following question: "**If you could choose one word to describe your emotions today, what would you choose and why?**" Keep it short by limiting answers to about 30 to 60 seconds each. Thank each participant for sharing before moving on to the next participant.

3. **BIBLE WORK**

❑ Going around the circle, invite participants to share a quick recap of how they did with their bible work by asking the following question, **"How did you do with your Bible scriptures and journaling?"** Keep it short by limiting answers to about 30 to 60 seconds each. Thank each participant for sharing before moving on to the next participant.

❑ Encourage participants to continue reading the Bible and journaling as part of their griefwork.

4. **DISCUSSION: What do we believe?**

❑ **LIFE & DEATH.** When we lose a loved one, their physical demise can challenge what we believe about life and death. Using the handout **WHAT DO I BELIEVE?**, guide the discussion by asking, **"What do you believe is the purpose of life? How did the loss of your loved one confirm or challenge what you believed?"** Allow each participant to answer then thank him/her for sharing before moving on to the next participant.

❑ **FAITH.** Those with a steadfast faith can be comforted or disappointed by the belief system they've adopted or been raised with. Using the handout **FAITH & DEATH,** guide the discussion by asking, **"How has your faith been impacted by the death of your loved one? Has it been a source of comfort or disappointment for you?"** Allow each participant to answer then thank him/her for sharing before moving on to the next participant.

5. **RESILIENCE RX**

❑ Remind participants of the importance of self-care as part of their griefwork. Going around the circle, invite participants to share a quick recap of how they did with their care plan by asking the following question, **"How did you do with your care plans?"**

❑ Invite them to review this session's handout and consider including it in their care plan.

6. **CONCLUSION**

Thank participants for coming and investing in their own well-being. Encourage them to:
❑ Read or review the session handouts
❑ Continue Bible work and journaling
❑ Add one activity to their self-care plan
❑ If desired, you can end with a poem, prayer, or group hug

SESSION 6 | HANDOUT 30

WHAT DO I BELIEVE?

When we lose a loved one, their physical demise can challenge what we believe about death. Christian mourners believe in heaven while others believe that when you're dust, you're dust. Further, our loved one's death can challenge what we believe is the purpose of life.

COMMON BELIEFS

- I believe we're here to learn lessons.
- I believe we're here to help others.
- I believe that everything happens for a reason, I just don't know what it is.

- I believe we have a preordained destiny.
- I believe there is no reason why we're here. It's purely natural evolution.
- I really don't know what I believe.

CASES TO PONDER

Certain deaths can challenge what we believe. Consider the following true losses:

- A wife found her 53-year-old husband deceased after he went to take a nap. Was her discovery of his deceased body somehow a lesson for her?

- A husband lost his 36-year-old wife to a drunk driver. Was her untimely death just part of life?

- A mother of four died by suicide following her divorce. Was her suicide part of their destiny?

- A 16-year-old lost his twin brother after they both fell in a frozen lake. Was there a lesson in it for the surviving twin?

- A mother of two lost both her kids in a car accident on an icy road. Was there a reason this mother became childless?

- A mother gave birth to a child who died of Trisomy 18. Was it for the best?

ANSWER THE FOLLOWING QUESTION

Without judgment, what do you believe about the purpose of life? How did the loss of your loved one confirm or challenge what you believed?"

SESSION 6 | HANDOUT 31

THE PURPOSE OF LIFE

WE DON'T LEARN FROM THE EASY STUFF

I was asked this morning by a dear friend what the purpose of life is. Why is it that some people face more heartache than seems fair?

Life unfolds differently for each of us. I personally believe we're here to learn lessons for our own growth. We don't learn from the easy stuff, and great challenges often yield the deepest lessons.

> Why, then, do some people go through life unscathed while others suffer greatly?

Sometimes we are the pupil meant to learn something from our own suffering. Sometimes we are the teacher imparting wisdom to those who witness our suffering.

When faced with great challenges, we have two options. One is to resist the change and stay outside immersed in the storm. Two is to surrender to something we can't change, and tend to our wound inside through the comfort of Christ.

Once the storm has passed and the wound less raw, we can re-enter life using the wisdom we learned.

Because God gave us all free will, you are the author of your own life story. Every sentence, paragraph, and page from cover to cover.

What do you want to write what has yet to be written?

You alone get to decide.

My answer to the question about the purpose of life is that it's a glorious yet mysterious classroom.

> Sometimes we're the pupil and sometimes the teacher.

It's up to each of us what we teach and learn.

LYNDA CHELDELIN FELL
H31/THE PURPOSE OF LIFE

FAITH & DEATH

Faith can be a source of comfort or disappointment after a loved one dies. Some mourners lean into their faith while others question the belief system they've adopted or been raised with. Some churches support mourners while others offer little or nothing to support the grief journey.

CASES TO PONDER

A mother who lost her 4-year-old son said, "I consider myself doubly blessed that in addition to my relationship with my husband growing stronger in the aftermath of our son's death, so has my relationship with God."

A father who lost his 1-year-old son said, "What was the point if God was to take my child? How can someone I've prayed to for most of my life, someone I trusted to always guide me and help me, take my firstborn?"

A sister who lost her 21-year-old brother to suicide said, "Prior to my brother's death I considered myself a person of faith. I have since lost my connection to faith, as the questions about where my brother has gone haven't been answered."

A mother who lost her 13-year-old daughter said, "My faith has never wavered. If anything, the accident has strengthened my faith even further and has provided an incredible source of comfort that I'm grateful for."

A husband who lost his 36-year-old wife said, "My view of what I saw Christians do and say has changed me. I wasn't prepared for losing seventy percent of our friends. When I went to church, they couldn't look me in the eye."

A mother who lost her 5-year-old daughter said, "I despised the saying 'bad things happen to good people.' It was a feeble attempt made by others to console and comfort me. Yet it never did. There was no reason, no plan for her to die. It just happened. Did God do it? Was I being punished for things in my past? Was I a bad parent? Where was God in this?"

ANSWER THE FOLLOWING QUESTION

Without judgment, how has your faith been impacted by the death of your loved one? Has it been a source of comfort or disappointment?

GOD'S SCRIPT

On the night of the accident, I sat next to my daughter's body at the scene of the two-car collision. As I sought to find her hand under the white sheet, God handed me a new script. I handed it back.

I wanted my old life, not a new one.

I wanted my daughter to open her eyes, to say "Hi, Mom."

Surveying the car's damage, instinctively I knew that wasn't going to happen. Yet shock, and the horror of seeing my daughter's bare toes peeking out from under the stark white sheet protected my mind from reality.

God again handed me the new script. I tore it up and handed it back.

"I don't want your new script!" I yelled.

I had a wonderful life as a mother of one college graduate, one college student, and two teenagers. My hubby and I were even blessed with our first grandchild. Life was wonderful! There was no need for God to go changing it.

But I didn't win. God did. I had no choice but to take the new script.

I ignored it for three years. And then tragedy struck again.

My dear hubby's grief consumed him, and he suffered a life-threatening stroke that left him disabled. He was just 46 years old.

I gave in and waved the white flag. There was nothing left of me. I was done. Exhausted. Here I was facing a new kind of grief, and I had hardly begun to process the first.

God's script laid there for months and months. My heart broken in so many places, I had no energy to read it. The lines blurred together, the words indistinguishable.

And then one day out of anger, I picked it up.

The first line said, "When you help others, you help your own heart to heal."

Seriously, God? I felt like a regressed teenager challenging a parent. I could hardly put one foot in front of the other, how was I supposed to help someone else?

But God didn't include instructions. I wasn't amused.

Yet I needed God. Desperately.

I gave in and waved the white flag. I was standing squarely in the belly of hell; I had nothing more to lose.

I wasn't entirely sure how to go about this new script, but herein lies the answer: I didn't have to figure it out all on my own.

One door opened, then two doors, then four. And so on and so forth.

It's now been seven years since the loss of our daughter and four years since my husband's life-changing stroke. I haven't figured it all out yet, but God's script gave me a life purpose far better than I could ever have imagined.

Where am I now? Today, I help others. Because this helps my own heart to heal.

There. I said it. Script accepted. God was right.

Helping others has come in many forms. One of my most joyous endeavors was creating the series *Grief Diaries*, an anthology of stories about surviving loss.

When I set out to compile these stories, some questioned whether I had lost my final marble. Who would want to read tales of life's most challenging moments? Yet, God had laid this on my heart. And I trusted him.

I knew, without a shadow of a doubt, that the collection was going to change lives around the world.

I trusted God's script, and strangers I've never met handed me the most precious of gift of all: their own loss experiences.

They entrusted me to handle each with kid gloves, package them oh-so-carefully, and present them to the world for the sole purpose of helping others not feel so alone. Each stranger became my friend who enriched my world beyond measure.

So, I no longer questioned the script. I just followed it, never once forgetting that every story I now held in the palm of my hand is sacred. Not just to the writer, but to the world.

And to God.

Suddenly, this crazy book series about sharing true stories about loss has given a platform to more than 700 writers around the world.

It feels good to share our experiences with others. Why? Because it helps both readers and writers feel less alone.

So, it's true. When we help others, we help our own heart to heal.

Baring and sharing to comfort others like ourselves. Healing hearts by sharing journeys.

Script accepted.

Thank you, God.

LYNDA CHELDELIN FELL (2016)
H33/GOD'S SCRIPT

RESILIENCE RX TIP 6

DANCE/MOVEMENT THERAPY

Feelings can influence our movement, and movement can impact our feelings. When we feel tired and sad, we tend to move slowly.

WHY IT WORKS

Moving our body improves our mood, helps combat anxiety and depression, and promotes a safe space for the expression of feeling.

Dancing is also emotionally therapeutic when paired with music we love. Since movement can be related to our thoughts and feelings, dancing benefits us physically and mentally through stress reduction, mood management, decreased muscle tension, increased mobility and more.

Further, it oxygenates the brain, which helps clear the mind and allows you to focus better.

PHYSICAL BENEFITS

Unlike the circulatory systems, the lymphatic system—the body's defense mechanism that fights illness—does not have a pump. It relies on large muscle movement to circulate the fluid that contains infection-fighting white blood cells around the body. Each time we dance, it helps pump lymphatic fluid through our body, keeping our systems circulating.

TAKE A RECESS

School recess was invented for a reason. Research shows that movement improves

HELPFUL TIP

Put on music you love, and dance for three minutes every day. If you feel inhibited, dance in the shower, your bedroom, or a private corner of your garden.

cognitive performance for people of all ages. Moving and dancing offer a mental recess through physical release.

Movement is one of the most basic functions of the human body, making it easy to incorporate motion into daily life in a way that feels good. If dancing isn't your thing, try one of the alternatives below.

ALTERNATIVE OPTIONS TO DANCING:

- ✓ Shake a bed sheet
- ✓ Run in place or jump up and down
- ✓ Stretch your large muscles
- ✓ Go for a walk
- ✓ Window shop
- ✓ Garden
- ✓ Clean a closet
- ✓ Grocery shop with a basket instead of a cart
- ✓ Romp around with the kids or grandkids
- ✓ Go hiking
- ✓ Take a bike ride

R08/RESILIENCE RX-DANCE/MOVEMENT THERAPY

BIBLE WORK

What does the Bible say about the purpose of life?

Many are the plans in a person's heart, but it is the Lord's purpose that prevails.

PROVERBS 19:21

SCRIPTURES TO EXPLORE

- ❏ JOB 42:2
- ❏ PROVERBS 16:4
- ❏ JEREMIAH 29:11
- ❏ PSALM 33:11

Losing a loved one causes many to question the purpose of life, especially a life cut short. After all, our purpose in life is the very meaning of our existence. In times of great sorrow, we can't help but wonder whether our loved one's life mattered. Does every life young and old have an impact on the world around us? Does every life hold meaning?

In the Bible, we're reassured that the Lord has a plan for us, a future, and that the plans of the Lord stand firm forever. In **Ephesians 2:10**, we're told that we are God's handiwork, created in Christ Jesus to do good works, which God prepared in advance for us to do. In **Acts 13:36**, we're told that when David had served God's purpose, he fell asleep and was buried with his ancestors where his body decayed.

If it is the duty of all mankind to keep God's commandments, what purpose does the death of a child hold? Does God have a purpose for a loved one who died by suicide? Is a premature death at the hands of an overdose or an accident some kind of punishment, or do we trust there are invisible lessons to be had that only God himself knows about?

WHAT DOES THE BIBLE SAY ABOUT THE PURPOSE OF LIFE?

Does the Bible's portrayal of our purpose bring comfort? If so, what scriptures do you find helpful?

ANSWER:

MY SCRIPTURES

Be the light
Ephesians 5:8

PRAYER

Dear God,

I can't help but wonder what purpose my loved one's life held. Did you send them to earth only to die so others could learn lessons from their death, from our suffering? Why does one person have to suffer so much while others skate through life?

Lord, I thank you for the knowledge that we are each created for a reason, that you have a divine purpose for each of us. I ask you to help me remember that my loved one's life held purpose—that we all hold purpose—and help me to let go and trust your bigger picture for us all. Lord, I ask that your will be done in my life.

In Jesus' name I pray, Amen.

A LETTER TO GOD

TODAY'S DATE: _____

Dear God,

iCare

J29/A LETTER TO GOD

SESSION 7

FINDING COMFORT

IC07/SESSION 7 INSTRUCTIONS

SESSION FORMAT

This session focuses on exploring what brings us comfort, how our needs may change over time, and also exploring the concept of gratitude for the collateral blessings that may reveal themselves along the grief journey. By verbalizing and sharing their own experiences and perspectives, mourners can learn from one another.

Following is this session's format:

1. Welcome and opening of session
2. Emotional check-in
3. Bible work check-in
4. Topic discussion
5. Review of self care
6. Conclusion

FACILITATION REMINDERS:

✓ Keep conversation moving. Protect conversation from being monopolized.

✓ Ensure every participant has an opportunity to answer the question. If the conversation jumps around the circle, be sure to circle back to those participants who haven't yet answered.

✓ If tension or disagreements flare during the discussion, reminder participants that this is a judgment-free zone and all perspectives are welcome.

✓ Stay neutral yet supportive.

LET'S BEGIN

1. **OPEN THE MEETING.**

   ❏ Ask everyone to take a seat and then welcome them back to session #7. Thank them for investing in their future by being there.

FORMS & HANDOUTS

❏ **FORM**: My Participants
❏ **FORM**: Sign-in sheet
❏ HANDOUT 36: Finding comfort
❏ HANDOUT 37: Collateral blessings
❏ HANDOUT 38: Finding an outlet
❏ HANDOUT 39: Why giving is good for the giver
❏ HANDOUT 40: Resilience Rx: Laugh therapy
❏ HANDOUT 41: Bible work

MATERIALS

❏ Workbooks
❏ Handouts
❏ Notebook & pen
❏ Nametags (if needed)
❏ Tissue
❏ Community resources
❏ Refreshments

2. EMOTIONAL CHECK-IN

❑ Going around the circle, ask participants one at a time the following question: **"If you could choose one word to describe your emotions today, what would you choose and why?"** Keep it short by limiting answers to about 30 to 60 seconds each. Thank each participant for sharing before moving on to the next participant.

3. BIBLE WORK

❑ Going around the circle, invite participants to share a quick recap of how they did with their bible work by asking the following question, **"How did you do with your Bible scriptures and journaling?"** Keep it short by limiting answers to about 30 to 60 seconds each. Thank each participant for sharing before moving on to the next participant.

❑ Encourage participants to continue reading the Bible and journaling as part of their griefwork.

4. DISCUSSION: **Finding comfort**

❑ **COMFORT.** What brings us comfort one day might irritate us the next. Using the handout **FINDING COMFORT?**, guide the discussion by asking, **"Has your comfort needs changed over time? What brings you comfort today?"** Allow each participant to answer then thank him/her for sharing before moving on to the next participant.

❑ **COLLATERAL BLESSINGS.** After loss, the grief journey can sometimes reveal silver linings that may not have come about any other way. Using the handout **COLLATERAL BLESSINGS**, guide the discussion by asking, **"Have you seen a silver lining or discovered a collateral blessing from your loss?"** Allow each participant to answer then thank him/her for sharing before moving on to the next participant.

5. RESILIENCE RX

❑ Remind participants of the importance of self-care as part of their griefwork. Going around the circle, invite participants to share a quick recap of how they did with their care plan by asking the following question, **"How did you do with your care plans?"**

❑ Invite them to review this session's handout and consider including it in their care plan.

6. CONCLUSION

Thank participants for coming and investing in their own well-being. Encourage them to:

❑ Read or review the session handouts

❑ Journal their thoughts

❑ Add one activity to their self-care plan

❑ If desired, you can end with a poem, prayer, or group hug

SESSION 7 | HANDOUT 36

FINDING COMFORT

When we lose someone we love, we have no idea where the journey will take us and what we'll need along the way. What feels comforting today might feel irritating tomorrow. Like most of the grief journey, there is no rhyme or reason to the ways we find comfort.

COMMON COMFORT ITEMS & ACTIVITIES

Holding their possessions. Holding a loved one's favorite pillow, stuffed animal, blanket or other treasured trinket allows us to feel close to him/her when it's in our hands.

Wearing their stuff. Wearing our loved one's bathrobe, shirts, watch, jewelry or sweatpants often bring comfort.

Personalize it. Gifts adorning our loved one's name or photo often bring comfort. Consider an ornament or a locket containing your loved one's photo, a bracelet engraved with their name, or a keychain adorned with your loved one's thumbprint.

Books & Audio. Grief books such as the *Grief Diaries* series reassure us we're not alone. A CD or playlist of our loved one's favorite songs can bring great comfort. Meditation apps can soothe raw nerves.

Silence. Stillness, quietness, and meditation can help us feel safe and grounded.

Familiarity. Eating our loved one's favorite food, watching their favorite movie, and going through their memorabilia can bring great comfort.

Expressive writing. Penning is useful for those who fear they'll forget the little things. Writing them down gives us a place to safely store our memories and ease the fear of forgetting moments we treasured.

Aromatherapy. Essential and fragrance oils have proven to calm our mood. Consider soothing candles, diffusers, jewelry diffusers, luxury soap, bath oils, potpourris, etc.

Pets. Interaction with our pets has been scientifically proven to reduce anxiety and lift our spirits in a safe, nonjudgmental way.

Gift of Comedy. It's been said that one laugh scatters a hundred griefs. A healthy dose of laughter can provide an emotional release that deserves recognition.

ANSWER THE FOLLOWING QUESTIONS

What brings you comfort today? Has this changed over time?

iCare

COLLATERAL BLESSINGS

Loss changes our lives. It changes who we are, where we are going, our relationships, and even how we look at life. It changes our priorities and often puts life into perspective. The idea that collateral blessings can come from a loved one's death can be shocking to some, and yet it's a common experience for many mourners. Sometimes the silver lining is small, other times it can catapult us in a positive new direction. Consider the following cases.

CASES TO PONDER

A mother who lost her daughter in a car crash said, "Losing our youngest daughter brought my oldest daughter and I closer. We used to be like oil and water. Now we're best friends."

A mother who lost her daughter to multiple congenital defects said, "My silver lining is that I will never wish to have her back. I miss her terribly, but never would I want her to come back to living with her multiple disabilities."

One father who lost his young son to drowning said, "My relationships with my mother and brothers are better. I didn't have this realization until I had to think about it."

A young woman who lost her father said, "The silver lining comes and goes. Some days it's bright and I'm filled with gratitude. Other times it's hidden behind the storm."

A husband who lost his wife to suicide said, "I haven't found a silver lining just yet, maybe because my grief is still so new."

A man who lost his brother to overdose said, "I don't take time for granted. I tell everyone I love, 'I love you.' My relationships have become deeper and more meaningful."

A young wife who lost her husband to cancer said, "I'm sure that some people who are new to their grief wonder how there could be a silver lining. It took years before I realized that there were good things in my life that would not be there if not for my husband's deaths.

A father who lost his son to an asthma attack said, "Unbelievably, there are many silver linings that have come to me. For years I was certain my life would not have any great meaning, nor did I care. I've learned that life can hold more than we could have imagined.

ANSWER THE FOLLOWING QUESTIONS

What collateral blessings have you found in your journey?

SESSION 7 | HANDOUT 38

FINDING AN OUTLET

WHY IT MATTERS

The brain can't tell the difference between physical and emotional pain, making it very important to engage in activities that give your brain a respite from the grief and help you to engage in life.

Further, studies show that performing a repetitive action with your hands required for such things as gardening, coloring, woodworking, kneading dough, beading, or doing yarnwork such as knitting or crocheting, induces a meditative state, calms your mood, and can even result in a new craft or gifts to give.

> ### HELPFUL TIP
>
> When grieving, it can feel as if everything in life has changed, and often it has. Creativity can be a solid, comforting, and familiar friend—a pillar of self-support.

Gallup conducted a study that showed people who use their gifts to help others experience the same benefits of giving. You get to exercise your talent and receive all the benefits of giving while others benefit from the giving of your talent. You can also use your outlet to validate and strengthen personal competency.

SUGGESTIONS:

- Learn to mold chocolate
- Learn to make soap
- Bead, knit, crochet, or quilt
- Volunteer in the community
- Learn a new sport such as golf
- Create a garden in a forgotten part of the yard

- Join Pinterest or a book club
- Doodle, draw, or mold clay
- Crochet a prayer shawl
- Sew a memorial quilt
- Join a community choir
- Read to children at the library
- Translate for a community organization

WHY GIVING IS GOOD FOR THE GIVER

I was asked by a mourner who was fresh into his journey why I advocate for the bereaved to give to others as a way to heal. After all, in the midst of autopilot, brain fog, and feeling utterly depleted before even getting out of bed, most mourners have nothing left to give.

So, here's my explanation on why giving is good for the giver.

When one suffers a broken leg, it takes time for the body to heal. The fracture scar will always be there because once done, it can't be undone, but strengthening the muscles and tissue around the break will help protect from further damage and promote healing.

Just like physical therapy is to broken bones, giving while grieving is therapy for the broken heart.

It releases powerful endorphins—a natural high, which are like little happy pills for brain pain.

The endorphins triggered by the act of intentional giving are also good for our body by reducing common grief banes—stress, anxiety and insomnia.

Does giving cure grief? No.

Losing someone we love causes grief that cannot be undone. It is something we learn to live with moving forward. But we can soothe the rawness and strengthen our broken heart through activities and actions such as giving.

What can you give when you feel empty inside?

- ✓ Give blood.
- ✓ Give a smile.
- ✓ Give a genuine compliment.
- ✓ Give blessing bags to the homeless.
- ✓ Give a car room to merge during rush hour.
- ✓ Give time at a homeless shelter, which serves as a powerful reminder that we're not alone on the struggle bus.
- ✓ Give a hug.

Winston Churchill once said, "We make a living by what we get. We make a life by what we give."

In other words, helping others helps our own heart to heal. It truly does.

LYNDA CHELDELIN FELL
H39/WHY GIVING IS GOOD FOR THE GIVER

SESSION 7 | HANDOUT 40

RESILIENCE RX

LAUGH THERAPY

Those who need a good laugh are usually the ones who feel least like laughing, yet the heart can hold joy the same time as sorrow, so go ahead and laugh. One laugh can scatter a hundred griefs, and help lift your spirits.

Even in difficult times, a laugh—or even simply a smile—can go a long way.

WHY IT MATTERS

Laughter creates the perfect diaphragmatic breath that oxygenates the brain. It also stimulates the brain into a positive state, which helps clear the mind and allows you more clarity and focus. When you're having a tough time, laughing creates psychological distance and can slow the momentum of overwhelm, frustration or disappointment.

A powerful healing modality, studies show that laughter offers many physical, psychological, and emotional benefits. Smiling and laughter stimulate the facial muscles that trigger the brain to release happy hormones called endorphins, the body's natural feel-good chemicals that promote an overall sense of well-being, temporarily relieves pain, decreases stress, and increases immune and infection-fighting antibodies.

BENEFITS OF LAUGH THERAPY

Because the body can't tell the difference between a real or fake smile, hold a pencil between your teeth to "fake it until you make it." When you smile, the stimulation of the involved facial muscles trigger the brain to release the chemicals that cause the feeling of happiness. A phenomenon called facial feedback, this works even if you weren't feeling happy in the first place.

The brain can't tell the difference and will be tricked into releasing those feel-good chemicals.

WHY IT WORKS:

- Laughter and crying are like yin and yang, they both release energy.

- Laughing bypasses the mind and helps us keep a positive attitude.

- Laughter engages in perfect diaphragmatic breath. When we laugh, we exhale completely and then inhale completely, which oxygenates the brain and body. When our brains are fully oxygenated, our minds become calm and clear.

HELPFUL TIP

Enjoy a good belly laugh at least once every day to oxygenate the brain and trigger endorphins that help us feel good. Studies show that ten minutes of laughter is equivalent to thirty minutes on a cardio machine.

- Laughter releases endorphins which help us feel good. The combination of brain oxygenation and endorphins is like a Joyful cocktail.

- When we feel good and the mind is clear, we feel grounded and peaceful, less stress and less reactive.

- Laughter doesn't change reality but does help us cultivate a positive mental attitude.

- Be silly, be playful. Laughter is contagious and allows our inner child to come out.

- Fake laughter often turns into authentic laughter. The brain can't tell the difference, and the health benefits are the same.

HOW TO LAUGH WHEN YOU DON'T FEEL LIKE IT:

- Watch a comedy movie or TV show
- Watch funny YouTube videos
- Listen to children laughing
- Watch blooper reels on TV
- Read a funny book

- Try laugh yoga
- Look at funny pictures
- Read funny social media memes
- Listen to funny jokes

No matter how you choose to induce a good belly laugh, the bottom line is that whatever makes you laugh is truly good medicine.

R07/RESILIENCE RX-LAUGH THERAPY

SESSION 7 | HANDOUT 41

BIBLE WORK

What does the Bible say about life's silver linings?

Not only so, but we also glory in our sufferings, because we know that suffering produces; perseverance, character, and hope.

ROMANS 5:3-4

SCRIPTURES TO EXPLORE

- ☐ PHILIPPIANS 1:12-18
- ☐ ROMANS 8:28
- ☐ JOB 2:10
- ☐ JOB 42:10

The saying "There's a silver lining in every cloud" originated not in the Bible, but in a poem written by John Milton in 1634. A metaphor for optimism, it means that a negative may have a positive to it.

While every rainbow begins with rain, mourning a loved one has more than its fair share of overcast days, yet clouds often symbolize that God is near. Job is a good example of finding the silver lining in life's difficulties because, in the end, Job gained more than he lost. Yet, finding a silver lining isn't easy when we're in great sorrow.

The Bible tells us that God is good, and He will do good through the trial we're now enduring. **Romans 8:28** says that God loves those who are His children, and He works all things together for good for us. So that must mean that the tribulations in our lives are part of the working together of all things for good. Therefore, all trials and tribulations must have a divine purpose, which is a silver lining in itself.

Is it possible to find a silver lining in sorrow? What good can come from the death of our loved one? When we don't see anything positive rising from our loss, is it possible to still believe in the bigger picture of God's work?

WHAT DOES THE BIBLE SAY ABOUT TRIBULATIONS AND OPTIMISM?

Does the Bible's portrayal of optimism bring comfort? If so, what scriptures do you find helpful?

ANSWER:

MY SCRIPTURES

Be the light
Ephesians 5:8

PRAYER

Dear God,

I struggle to find optimism, as I don't see anything good that has come from my loved one's death. Please help me open my eyes and heart to the blessings that may arise from my loss.

Lord, I thank you for the knowledge that I was created to shine with your glory. I ask you to give me the energy to shine with all my might as a testament of my love for you, even in times of deep grief. I ask you to use my sorrow to help others struggling with their own.

In Jesus' name I pray, Amen.

A LETTER TO GOD

TODAY'S DATE: _____

Dear God,

_____

_____

_____

_____

_____

_____

_____

_____

_____

_____

_____

_____

_____

_____

_____

_____

I'm trusting the *Author* of my story

J29/A LETTER TO GOD

SESSION 8

HOPE & GRATITUDE

IC08/SESSION 8 INSTRUCTIONS

SESSION FORMAT

This session focuses on exploring the concept of hope after loss and the power of gratitude. By verbalizing and sharing their own perspectives, mourners can learn from and be inspired by one another.

Following is this session's format:

1. Welcome and opening of session
2. Emotional check-in
3. Bible work check-in
4. Topic discussion
5. Review of self care
6. Conclusion

FACILITATION REMINDERS:

✓ Keep conversation moving. Protect conversation from being monopolized.

✓ Ensure every participant has an opportunity to answer the question. If the conversation jumps around the circle, be sure to circle back to those participants who haven't yet answered.

✓ If tension or disagreements flare during the discussion, reminder participants that this is a judgment-free zone and all perspectives are welcome.

✓ Stay neutral yet supportive.

LET'S BEGIN

1. **OPEN THE MEETING.**

   ❑ Ask everyone to take a seat, open with the prayer on page 26 or one of your own, if desired, and then welcome them back to session #8. Thank them for investing in their future by being there.

FORMS & HANDOUTS

❑ **FORM**: My Participants

❑ **FORM**: Sign-in sheet

❑ HANDOUT 42: Is hope possible after loss?

❑ HANDOUT 43: The power of gratitude

❑ HANDOUT 44: My playbook of grief

❑ HANDOUT 45: When grief steals our technicolor

❑ HANDOUT 46: Turning pain into purpose

❑ HANDOUT 47: What now?

❑ HANDOUT 48: Resilience Rx: Hug therapy

❑ HANDOUT 49: Bible work

MATERIALS

❑ Workbooks

❑ Handouts

❑ Notebook & pen

❑ Nametags (if needed)

❑ Tissue

❑ Community resources

❑ Refreshments

2. EMOTIONAL CHECK-IN

❑ Going around the circle, ask participants one at a time the following question: **"If you could choose one word to describe your emotions today, what would you choose and why?"** Keep it short by limiting answers to about 30 to 60 second seconds each. Thank each participant for sharing before moving on to the next participant.

3. BIBLE WORK

❑ Going around the circle, invite participants to share a quick recap of how they did with their bible work by asking the following question, **"How did you do with your Bible scriptures and journaling?"** Thank each participant for sharing before moving on to the next participant.

❑ Encourage participants to continue reading the Bible and journaling as part of their griefwork.

4. DISCUSSION: Hope & Gratitude

❑ **HOPE.** It's been said that without grief, there would be no need for hope. Yet it's easy to feel robbed of all the things we had hoped for before our loved one died. Using the handout **IS HOPE POSSIBLE AFTER LOSS?**, guide the discussion by asking, **"What is your definition of hope? Has it changed since your loved one died?"** Allow each participant to answer then thank him/her for sharing before moving on to the next participant.

❑ **GRATITUDE.** After loss, it can be hard to find anything to be grateful for, and often isn't something we consciously think about. Using the handout **THE POWER OF GRATITUDE,** guide the discussion by asking, **"What are you thankful for today?"** Allow each participant to answer then thank him/her for sharing before moving on to the next participant.

5. RESILIENCE RX

❑ Remind participants of the importance of self-care as part of their griefwork. Going around the circle, invite participants to share a quick recap of how they did with their care plan by asking the following question, **"How did you do with your care plans?"**

❑ Invite them to review this session's handout and consider including it in their care plan.

6. CONCLUSION

Thank participants for coming and investing in their own well-being. Encourage them to:

❑ Review the session handouts from time to time

❑ Continue Bible work and journaling their thoughts moving forward

❑ Review their self-care plan every 3 months and freshen it up if needed

❑ If desired, begin closing ceremony or end this final session on a poem, prayer, or group hug

IS HOPE POSSIBLE AFTER LOSS?

It's been said that without grief, there would be no need for hope. Yet it's easy to feel robbed of all the things we had hoped for, including our loved one's future and how it once was intertwined with our own. As we learn to live with our loved one in our hearts instead of our arms, what does hope look like? Is it possible to feel hope and happiness ever again? What does the future hold?

CASES TO PONDER

A widowed wife said, "Hope is watching a sunset and knowing you made it through another day. Hope is knowing if you got through one day, you will get through another."

A widowed husband said, "My definition of hope is still somewhat the same: that life will get better even though the heartbreak will always be with me."

A young woman who lost her sister said, "My definition of hope is looking forward to better days. I look forward to being able to live again with peace, joy, strength, and happiness."

A father who lost his son said, "Whoever said hope has no fear has never been more right. I fear nothing. Life is going to happen whether I worry or not. To me, hope is that voice in my soul saying it's going to eventually be okay, so the next day I get up and try again."

A bereaved mother said, "What I hope for now has changed from material things to Bible things. This is a good thing."

A grandmother who lost her grandson said, "Hope is feeling the ability to navigate through difficult challenges and trust that I'll arrive at a better place."

A young man who lost his mother said, "Hope to me is finding a way to live a happy life and being able to deal with my mom's death. It is about learning to be happy with the memories, accepting the blessing of her being my mother and moving forward."

A bereaved mother said, "I wondered if I was forever going to feel lost. Would I ever smile and laugh again? Yes, it did happen. Now I accept my loss and finally am in a place of being able to feel joy again."

ANSWER THE FOLLOWING QUESTIONS

What is your definition of hope today? Have you found hope?

THE POWER OF GRATITUDE

WHY IT MATTERS

Physician and philosopher Albert Schweitzer said, "At times our own light goes out and is rekindled by a spark from another person. Each of us has cause to think with deep gratitude of those who have lit the flames within us."

While it can be hard to evolve gratitude when grieving someone we love, gratitude is an intentional mindset and powerful healing modality. Daily gratitude by consciously counting our blessings—a thankful appreciation for what we have—gets easier with practice. The more grateful we are, the more gratitude we have.

Begin by creating a Gratitude Jar and once daily write down either a collateral blessing—unexpected silver linings resulting from life challenges—or a blessing that you're grateful for and deposit it in the jar. In six months, revisit what you wrote and start a new gratitude jar. Continue the practice until instinctive gratitude returns to your heart.

CREATE A GRATITUDE JAR

- Once a day think about what you're grateful for.
- Have an open mind.
- Allow yourself to feel gratitude.
- Note your gratitude on a slip of paper.
- Add it to your jar.
- Share it with someone else, if desired.

ANSWER THE FOLLOWING QUESTION

What are you thankful for today?

_____

_____

_____

_____

_____

MY PLAYBOOK OF GRIEF

I didn't want to get out of bed this morning. Not because today marks nine years since losing my daughter, Aly. Rather, the feel of the cool sheets, my sleeping hubby next to me, and the warm sun filtering through our bedroom window felt too peaceful to disturb.

So, I laid there and allowed my mind to wander over the past nine years.

I replayed that night at the crash site when I sat next to Aly, how I held her warm hand while first responders on scene surrounded me with love. How my husband called for an update on the fender-bender only to learn that his beloved youngest daughter was covered by the stark white sheet of death.

How I made my way home as the full moon gave way to dawn, wondering when I'll wake from this nightmare.

What I didn't know then that I know now is that I would survive.

In those early days I didn't think I could endure grief's agony, and many days I didn't want to. The pain is beyond explanation, and can't be comprehended by simply reading about it in a college textbook.

How could I learn to live with my daughter in my heart instead of my arms?

I didn't know. But whether I liked it or not, I was about to learn.

My playbook of grief begins with a fog of shock so strong, I don't remember much. The next few chapters are filled with wailing, gnashing of teeth, and spewing vile words. I then embarked on a desperate search for comfort, for relief from the agony.

The end of my playbook remains unwritten but the rawness has softened and the current chapters teach that the heart can hold joy the same time as sorrow.

There are many lessons and chapters in my playbook, but the most surprising of all is the one about transformation.

In the early days, it's hard to believe grief is survivable, little alone transformative. How could we? We can't see past the pain.

But as our rawness softens and coping skills strengthen, we move into an unexpected—and for many, positive—transformative phase.

What I didn't know nine years ago that I know now is that my daughter's death was the gateway to many blessings.

My circle of friends has expanded to include strangers who speak all loss languages. This taught me that the foundation of mankind is love.

My skillset has expanded to things I didn't know I could do. This taught me that limitations are self induced, and I can do more than I think.

My compassion has grown in ways I could never have imagined. I learned to see outside my own pain into other hurting hearts, and how helping them helps my own heart to heal.

My gratitude has evolved into an intentional mindset. This taught me that being grateful is a powerful healing modality. The more grateful I am, the more gratitude I have.

Am I grateful for Aly's death?

No. It's a hellacious journey. But I am grateful for the collateral blessings. This taught me that there is more to grief than meets the eye.

Nine years ago I didn't want to live. But others held that light of hope when I had none. This taught me the importance of sparking, igniting, and shining our light for those in the darkness behind us.

I'm often asked whether the pain ever truly ends.

One cliché is that we don't get over grief, we move through it. I don't believe we move through it. I believe we carry it with us as we learn to move forward in life.

To answer the question, I do believe pain eases. If it can happen to me, it can happen to anyone. The timing might be different, but don't give up. It's worth fighting for.

Life's second act will be different, but enjoy the moments when the pain isn't as suffocating and you'll find that you don't have to choose between sorrow or joy. The heart has room for both, and eventually the joy will grow as the rawness softens.

Nine years ago I didn't believe I would survive losing Aly.

What I didn't know then that I know now is not only would I survive, I might actually like—no, love—life.

LYNDA CHELDELIN FELL (2018)

H44/MY PLAYBOOK OF GRIEF

HOLD ON PAIN EASES

SESSION 8 | HANDOUT 45

WHEN GRIEF STEALS OUR TECHNICOLOR

Years after losing my daughter, I was asked one day how I wake every morning with hope in my heart. I paused for a moment, searching for words, and then it came:

I fought for it.

You see, one morning after her death, while lying in bed I was engaged in the daily struggle of wanting to pull the covers over my head but knowing I needed to get up for my own good.

For a brief moment I allowed myself to simply lay there and listen to the birds sing outside my bedroom window. This was something I used to love to do, yet up until that moment, my daughter's death had robbed me of all joy.

The world continued on around me yet I failed to engage.

It was then when I realized that my whole world had become 50 shades of grey.

Grief had stolen the technicolor from my world, robbing me of the ability to appreciate much of anything.

Still in my forties, I realized that morning while lying in bed that I had a choice to make: either find a way to begin living, or live my remaining years robbed of all joy.

Because hope and happiness are intertwined like peanut butter and jelly, in order to restore happiness, I had to find hope.

From that moment forward, I made the effort to appreciate life's beauty.

Although not every day is beautiful, there is beauty in every day if you look for it.

At first it was incredibly hard to allow my heart to see or feel anything besides my anguish, but determined, I forged on.

I fought hard.

It took time. Patience.

And great effort.

But it paid off.

My world slowly began to fill with hope, beauty, and gratitude.

There are no good analogies when it comes to grief, but when you're lost in the middle of nowhere, you can wait for help to arrive or start walking toward civilization. It's okay to cry along the way and rest when you need to, but keep walking. And Keep fighting.

Hope and happiness are on the horizon.

And they're both worth fighting for.

LYNDA CHELDELIN FELL
H45/WHEN GRIEF STEALS OUR TECHNICOLOR

iCare

TURNING PAIN INTO PURPOSE

My story began one night in 2007, when I had a vivid dream. I was the front passenger in a car and my daughter Aly was sitting behind the driver. Suddenly the car missed a curve and sailed into a lake. The driver and I escaped the sinking car, but Aly did not.

My beloved daughter was gone. The only thing she left behind was a book floating in the water where she disappeared.

Two years later, in August 2009, that horrible nightmare came true when Aly died as a back seat passenger in a car accident.

Returning home from a swim meet, the car carrying Aly was T-boned by a father coming home from work. My beautiful fifteen-year-old daughter took the brunt of the impact and died instantly. She was the only fatality.

Life couldn't get any worse, right? Wrong. Hell wasn't done with me yet.

My dear hubby buried his grief in the sand. He escaped into 80-hour work weeks, more wine, more food, and less talking. His blood pressure shot up, his cholesterol went off the chart, and the perfect storm arrived on June 4, 2012.

Out of the blue, my husband suddenly began drooling and was unable to talk. At age 46, my soulmate was having a major stroke.

My dear hubby lived, but he couldn't talk, read, or write, and his right side was paralyzed. He needed help just to sit up in bed. He needed full-time care.

Still reeling from the loss of our daughter, I once again found myself thrust into a fog of grief so thick, I couldn't see through the storm. Autopilot resumed its familiar place at the helm.

I needed God and was desperate for reassurance that the sun was on the other side of hell. As I fought my way through the storm, God showed me that helping others was a powerful way to heal my own heart. I began reaching out to individuals who were adrift and in need of a warm hug.

In 2013, I formed AlyBlue Media to house my mission. Comforting people who spoke my language and listening to their stories, my mission took on a life of its own and came in many forms: a radio show, film, webinars, and writing. I also hosted a national convention. I wanted to bring the brokenhearted together.

I had many wonderful speakers, but the one who excited me most was a woman who had faced seven losses in a few short years—Martin Luther King's youngest daughter.

I didn't bring Dr. Bernice King to the convention to tell us about her famous father—we already knew that story. I wanted to know how she survived.

Over the course of that weekend, I was deeply moved by watching strangers swap stories and become newfound friends. These were stories born from hardship and yet remarkable on many levels.

Touched to the core, I set out to capture them into a book series aptly named Grief Diaries.

Now home to seven literary awards and more than 700 writers spanning the globe, Grief Diaries has 35 titles in print. Two years later I founded the International Grief Institute to help others invest in community resilience and strengthen the pipeline of hope.

I wanted to be a brain surgeon, but God had other plans. Being thrown into the forge so He could mold my soul was necessary for Him to accomplish those plans.

Life's lessons aren't easy because as humans, we don't learn from the easy stuff. It's sometimes necessary to reduce us like molten metal before we can be forged into a pillar of hope, courage, strength—or whatever God wants us to be—so we can serve others.

Once the forging was done, He filled my life—and heart—with blessings for which I am truly grateful, blessings that wouldn't have come about any other way.

Where am I today?

Once a bereaved mother, always a bereaved mother. My heart is a bit like a broken teacup that's been glued back together. All the pieces are there, but they might not fit as seamlessly as they once did.

Some days the glue is strong and unyielding. Others, that glue is soft and threatens to spring a leak. Nonetheless, that teacup still holds water and serves a purpose.

It's important to hold out hope that the sun can be found at the end of the path. But until you find it, it's comforting to know you aren't alone.

God is there, even when you don't think He is.

For the record, I've found the sun. Some days I marvel at its beauty. Other days it hides behind clouds. But I now know those days don't last forever. And thanks to the lessons I've learned from my loss and trusting God along the way, my umbrella is stronger than ever.

Long story short, if I can turn pain into purpose, you can too. Maybe not right this minute, but when God feels you're ready, He'll point you in the right direction.

Just trust that there is a bigger picture at play, and remember that He's not asking you to save the world, just help one person at a time.

In doing so, you'll help your own heart to heal.

LYNDA CHELDELIN FELL
H46/TURNING PAIN INTO PURPOSE

SESSION 8 | HANDOUT 47

WHAT NOW?

When a grief support group comes to an end, some are left wondering, "What now?"

Much like learning to ride a bike, finishing a support group is like removing the training wheels and trying to ride without them. Can you do it? Absolutely!

While the pain of your loss didn't magically go away, most participants leave a grief support group with new tools to help them continue their griefwork, and found comfort in knowing they weren't alone with their struggles.

ANSWER THE FOLLOWING QUESTIONS

Take stock at where you were before the support group began, and where you are now by answering the following questions.

- ❑ What did you expect from attending this support group?
- ❑ What did you learn about yourself by attending?
- ❑ What did you learn about grief?
- ❑ What did you learn from others experiencing grief?
- ❑ What did you learn about self-care? Are you willing to continue working on your self-care plan?

SESSION 8 | HANDOUT 48

RESILIENCE RX

HUG THERAPY

Giving is good for the giver in that a hug benefits both ourselves and others. A hug is a free, easy, and—at 20 seconds—a quick way to trigger endorphins, foster connections and show appreciation.

BENEFITS OF HUG THERAPY:

Almost 70 percent of communication is nonverbal. Hugging is an excellent method of expressing yourself nonverbally to another human or animal. Not only can they feel the love and care in your embrace, but they can actually be receptive enough to pay it back. And it's free every time we hug, cradle a child, cherish a dog or cat, slow dance, or simply hold the shoulders of a friend.

A sincere embrace triggers the brain to release the love hormone known as oxytocin. This substance has many benefits. A natural tranquilizer that's released during childbirth, oxytocin is powerful enough to help mothers forget about the labor they endured and fall immediately in love with their newborn. It's not just for new mothers, though. Oxytocin helps everyone to relax and feel safe. It also calms our fears and anxiety. A neurotransmitter that acts on the brain's emotional center, oxytocin is known to promote contentment, reduce anxiety, lower our heart rate and our cortisol level, a stress hormone.

HUGS ALSO . . .

Affection also has a direct response on the reduction of stress which prevents many diseases. Touch Research Institute at the University of Miami School of Medicine has carried out more than 100 studies on the power of touch, and discovered evidence of improved immune system, reduced pain and more.

✓ Hugs apply gentle pressure on the sternum which stimulates the thymus gland, which regulates the production of white blood cells, which keep you healthy.

✓ Hugs stimulate the brain to release the pleasure hormone dopamine, which helps to negate sadness.

✓ Hugging also releases serotonin levels, elevating mood and creating happiness.

✓ Skin contains a network of tiny pressure centers that sense touch and notify the brain through the vagus nerve. The skin response of someone receiving and giving a hug shows a change in skin conductance which suggests a more balanced state in the parasympathetic nervous system.

So go ahead . . . hug it out!

R06/RESILIENCE RX-HUG THERAPY

HELPFUL TIP

Research shows that a hug lasting at least 20 seconds has a therapeutic effect on the body and mind. Hug someone or something for at least 20 seconds every day.

BIBLE WORK

What does the Bible say about hope?

But as for me, I watch in hope for the Lord,
I wait for God my Savior, my God will hear me.

MICAH 7:7

SCRIPTURES TO EXPLORE

- ❑ JEREMIAH 29:11
- ❑ ROMANS 15:13
- ❑ ISAIAH 41:10
- ❑ PSALM 62:5

When a loved one dies, it's common to feel hopeless, that we have nothing left to live for. Yet, in **Romans 12:12**, we're told to rejoice in hope, be patient in tribulation, be constant in prayer. **Hebrews 11:1** tells us that faith is the assurance of things hoped for, the conviction of things not seen. **Romans 8:24-25** also tells us to wait with patience for hope for what we do not see.

The story of Daniel walking into the lion's den with the odds stacked against him is perhaps one of the greatest stories of hope overcoming despair. In **Daniel 6**, the ruler Darius the Mede was tricked by Daniel's rivals into issuing a decree that for thirty days no prayers should be addressed to any god or man but Darius himself. Anyone who disobeyed was to be thrown to the lions. Defying the order, Daniel continued to pray to God. Condemned for his actions, Daniel was thrown to a certain death at the jaws of the lions, but instead was found alive in the morning, as God had protected him from the lions' jaws.

When we're in despair, do we pray God will restore our hope, our faith, or both?

WHAT DOES THE BIBLE SAY ABOUT HOPE?

Does the Bible's portrayal of hope bring comfort?
If so, what scriptures do you find helpful?

ANSWER:

_____

_____

_____

MY SCRIPTURES

_____

_____

_____

_____

Be the light
Ephesians 5:8

PRAYER

Dear God,

This journey through sorrow has been long and hard. I am told to wait with patience for hope, yet I'm not even sure what to hope for.

Lord, I thank you for walking with me on this journey, and for reminding me that you created me for good works. I trust that my season of grief will lead to new growth, and you'll turn my pain into purpose that gives me hope and glorifies you when you're ready.

In Jesus' name I pray, Amen.

A LETTER TO GOD

TODAY'S DATE: _____

Dear God,

iCare

CHAPTER 8
CLOSING CEREMONY

Grieving doesn't stop when funeral services end.

SHERRY DEE MOBLEY

A closing ceremony is a powerful remembrance ritual that offers participants a symbolic release at the end of their sessions together, and a memory they'll treasure.

A closing ceremony can take any form, and be led by either one or two facilitators. The following format uses one facilitator. In general, the ceremony includes music, prayers and/or poems, and candles. Modify as needed.

PLAN

1. Allow 20 to 30 minutes at the end of your final group session for the closing ceremony.

2. Confirm whether use of lit candles is allowed within the facility. If not, consider LED candles or glowsticks.

3. Assemble the following prayers and/or poems:
   a. Opening prayer or poem
   b. Five Candles poem on next page
   c. Another poem, if desired
   d. Closing prayer or poem (consider *Time Will Ease the Hurt* on the next page).

4. Secure music, device to play it on, and Bluetooth speaker if needed. See song suggestions on page 167.

5. Consider purchasing or making trinkets bearing each participant's loved one's name to give as keepsakes (look at My Participants form or Registration form for loved one's names). Visit your local dollar store for supplies or visit www.Etsy.com for ideas if you don't want to make your own. Consider personalized ornaments, keychains, bookmarks, or other inexpensive ideas to keep costs down.

MATERIALS

- ❑ Refreshments
- ❑ 5 votive candles with glass holders
- ❑ Church candles (one for every participant plus facilitators)
- ❑ Wax catchers for each church candle
- ❑ Bucket of water
- ❑ Matches or lighter
- ❑ Music
- ❑ Bluetooth speaker, if needed
- ❑ Poems or prayers
- ❑ Table décor, if desired
- ❑ Tissue
- ❑ OPTIONAL: Keepsake ornament or trinket bearing loved ones' name for each participant to take home

PREPARE

- ❏ Purchase candles with wax catchers from a religious store, or arts & crafts store. Assemble candles inside wax catchers prior to ceremony. Don't forget matches or lighter.

- ❏ If using a cell phone for music, pair a portable Bluetooth speaker with your phone ahead of time. Find a volume setting that's loud enough to hear but doesn't drown out the facilitator's voice. TIP: If you have a second facilitator, his/her role can be to adjust music volume.

- ❏ Purchase or find donated cookies and bottled water or coffee to serve afterward.

- ❏ Secure bucket of water for participants to drop candles in when finished.

- ❏ Prepare keepsake ornaments or trinkets, if desired.

SUGGESTED SCHEDULE

1. Prior to ceremony, set up a row of five unlit votive candles on a table. Decorate the table if desired.

2. Begin with facilitator reciting opening prayer and/or poem.

3. Facilitator comments: Thank participants for investing in themselves by attending the support group, and share the importance of continuing their griefwork through Bible work, care plans, and engaging with local grief resources. Keep this short, no longer than 2 to 3 minutes.

4. Start music. While music is playing, facilitator lights his/her own candle using a match or lighter. TIP: If desired, prior to ceremony ask one participant to light your candle when cued instead of lighting your candle yourself.

5. Adjust music volume down, facilitator then reads the **Five Candles** poem (see next page) loud enough for all to hear while lighting each of the five corresponding candles on the table.

6. Facilitator then invites participants one at a time to dip their candlewick into facilitator's flame to light their own candle while saying their loved one's name. You can say. "One at a time, please dip your candle into my flame while saying your loved one's name. Then hold out your hand to receive a keepsake to remember our time together."

   Allow each participant to say their loved one's name as they light their own candle, then gently place a keepsake bearing their loved one's name into their hand before the next participant lights his/her candle, says their loved one's name, etc.

7. After all candles are lit, facilitator may recite another prayer or poem if desired.

8. Allow the music to finish, then ask for a moment of silence. TIP: Can play one song on a loop or add a second song if needed until every participant has lit their candle and said loved one's name.

9. Facilitator ends with closing prayer or another poem.

10. Distinguish candles and dispose of them in bucket of water.

11. Invite participants to end with a group hug. TIP: Be sure all candles are extinguished prior to group hug to avoid lighting someone's hair on fire.

I09/CLOSING CEREMONY

SUGGESTED SONGS

- ❏ Somewhere Over the Rainbow
- ❏ I Will Always Love You, by Whitney Houston
- ❏ Amazing Grace
- ❏ To Where You Are, by Josh Groban
- ❏ Wind Beneath my Wings, by Bette Midler
- ❏ Go Light Your World, by C. Rice

SUGGESTED POEMS

FIVE CANDLES

UNKNOWN AUTHOR

The first candle represents our grief.
The pain of losing you is intense.
It reminds us of the depth of our love for you.

This second candle represents our courage.
To confront our sorrow,
To comfort each other,
To change our lives.

This third candle we light in your memory.
For the times we laughed,
The times we cried,
The times we were angry with each other,
The silly things you did,
The caring and joy you gave us.

This fourth candle we light for our love.
We light this candle that your light will always shine.
As we enter this season and share this night of remembrance with our family and friends.
We cherish the special place in our hearts that will always be reserved for you.

This fifth candle we light to thank you for the gift your living brought to each of us.

We love you.

We remember you.

TIME WILL EASE THE HURT

BY BRUCE B. WILMER

The sadness of the present days
is locked and set in time.
And moving to the future
is a slow and painful climb.

But all the feelings that
are now so vivid and real
can't hold their fresh intensity
as time begins to heal.

No wound so deep will
ever go entirely away,
yet every hurt becomes
a little less each day.

Nothing can erase the painful
imprints on your mind.
But there are softer memories
that time will let you find.

Though your heart won't let
the sadness simply slide away,
the echoes will diminish
even though the memories stay.

SUGGESTED POEMS (CONTINUED)

FOR MY COMPASSIONATE FRIENDS (child loss)

BY MARILYN ROLLINS, The Compassionate Friends, Lake-Porter County, Indiana

How is it that I know you?
How'd you get into my life?
Sometimes when I look at you,
It cuts me like a knife.

I do not want to know you,
I don't want to cross that line.
Let's both go back into the past,
When everything was fine.

You've held me and you've hugged me,
And dried a tear or two,
Yet, you're practically a stranger,
Why do you do the things you do?

Of course, I know the reason,
We are in this club we're in,
And why we hold on to each other
Like we are long lost kin.

For us to know each other,
We had to lose a kid,
I wish I'd never met you,
But, I'm so thankful that I did.

ADDITIONAL HANDOUTS

RESILIENCE RX™
Coping with grief at work

The wealth of a company is built on the health of its employees. When grief impacts our life, the emotional stress and mental exhaustion make us less organized, less productive, and less efficient. Emotional depletion can lead to other health problems such as insomnia, hypertension, and more. Use the tips below to manage grief when you return to work. Stay in contact with your boss or human resources to make sure they are supporting you in your time of need.

Self-compassion involves a consistent attitude of kindness and acceptance toward ourselves as a whole.

LISA FIRESTONE, Ph.D.

SELF CARE TIPS FOR WORK:

- Work with your employer to identify a safe room you can use for 5 to 10 minutes when emotions bubble to the surface. This gives you the space to collect yourself in a private setting away from clients and colleagues.
- Compartmentalize if needed at work but give yourself time to grieve, too.
- If possible, request short-term light cognitive duty to minimize the risk of mistakes and injuries.
- Avoid operating dangerous equipment until the fog lifts. This will maximize safety and minimize risk management issues.
- Learn to let go, say no, and ask for help from others. Honor your own limits.

SELF CARE TIPS FOR HOME:

- Talk about your loss for at least 15 minutes every day. It's okay to ramble, rant, and repeat yourself. Talking is how we process. Processing is how we heal.
- Carve time in your schedule to do things you love. This will help recharge your battery.
- Eat healthy and stay hydrated to boost immunity and physical well-being.
- Engage in light exercise and practice good sleep hygiene.
- Sing. In the shower, in the car, in your bed. It releases muscle tension and stress.
- Enjoy a good belly laugh every day. Laughter releases tension, boosts your mood, and lightens a heavy heart. Watch a comedy or funny videos.
- Engage in activities involving repetitive hand motions such as beading, painting, pottery, knitting, gardening, woodworking or coloring. Repetitive hand motions calms the mind.
- Use journaling to release inner thoughts and feelings.
- Recognize that you can't fix grief. It's a rite of passage for everyone.

RESILIENCE RX™
Coping with isolation

Dealing with social restrictions during a pandemic can create loneliness, isolation, stress and anxiety. You can help offset these feelings with things that give you a sense of control.

In the sweetness of friendship let there be laughter and sharing of pleasures.
KHALIL GIBRAN

TIPS

- Take a break from news to minimize trauma overload.

- Stay in the present. Think about right now and don't let your mind wander past the next 48 hours.

- If you find yourself in a spiral, spell your name backwards out loud to reground your thoughts.

- Stay on schedule to give yourself purpose.

  ◆ Take a virtual exercise class

  ◆ Try a new dinner recipe each night

- Focus on quality interactions regardless of physical proximity. Try a virtual happy hour with friends, daily or weekly Skypes with family and friends, online cultural or religious event or digital gatherings.

- Replace "social distancing" with "physical distancing" as a reminder that we're still connected.

- Jump into a project such as a jigsaw puzzle, woodworking, quilting, or soap making. It will help you stay busy, engaged, and productive.

- Curl up in your favorite chair and read a good book or watch an interesting TV series. When you're engaged in a good storyline, your brain produces dopamine — a hormone that promotes happiness.

REMINDERS

- ✓ Take one moment at a time.

- ✓ Be gentle with yourself.

- ✓ Crying is an appropriate response that helps release stress.

- ✓ Lethargy, exhaustion, forgetfulness and brain fog are normal stress responses.

- ✓ Give yourself lots of grace and practice staying in the present.

RESILIENCE RX™
EMDR Therapy

Eye Movement Desensitization and Reprocessing is an extensively researched psychotherapy modality developed by Dr. Francine Shapiro, a proponent of trauma-informed mental health care, who discovered a connection between eye movement and upsetting memories in the late 1980s. EMDR underwent its first clinical trial in 1989.

The thing that EMDR therapy does so beautifully is to remove the barrier so that the client can begin connecting the positives and safety of the present with the pain of the past. —DR. JIM KNIPE, psychologist

EMDR has been demonstrated to be an effective treatment for trauma and trauma-related disorders by helping the brain jumpstart its natural networking to process those experiences.

Now used around the world for disorders such as PTSD, anxiety, depression, and other sequelae of traumatic life experiences, research shows that EMDR reduces the vividness and emotions associated with the traumatic memories.

HOW IT WORKS

A typical EMDR therapy session with a trained mental health clinician lasts from 60-90 minutes.

The client is instructed to briefly focus on the traumatic memory while simultaneously moving the eyes in a specific way. During the eye movements, attention is first focused on a negative emotion, image, or body sensation related to this event, and then shifts to a positive belief.

While the experience isn't forgotten, the emotional response from the event is lessened or resolved.

8 PHASES

EMDR is divided into 8 phases that guide treatment:

1. History is discussed and treatment plan is developed

2. Preparation, explanation and EMDR expectations

3. Assessment of traumatic event

4. Desensitization technique

5. Installation of a positive belief

6. Body scan to check for lingering disturbance

7. Closure to return to calm

8. Re-evaluation at each subsequent session

RESILIENCE RX™
Forest Therapy

Forest therapy is rooted in the Japanese practice of Shinrin-yoku, which is often translated as "forest bathing." According to a 10-year study by Dr. Margaret Stroebe and Dr. Henk Schut, the Dual Process Model of Coping recommends a change of scenery as part of a healthy grief process.

There are moments when all anxiety and stated toil are becalmed in the infinite leisure and repose of nature. —HENRY DAVID THOREAU

BENEFITS

Nature offers one of the most reliable boosts to your mental and physical well-being. The natural environment is restorative, and studies demonstrate a wide array of health benefits, especially for stabilizing and improving mood and cognition.

Doses of nature from a walk outside can restore waning attention, improve concentration, decrease anxiety levels and improve your mood. Even looking at a natural scene through a window can help.

Forest bathing not only lowers production of stress hormones, it also influences our immune system. Natural chemicals secreted by evergreen trees known as phytoncide have been shown to improve our body's immune functions, which can be critical when we're emotionally under duress after losing a loved one.

EMOTIONAL CONNECTION

Stress, anxiety, and depression may all be eased by time outdoors, especially when combined with brisk movement or exercise. The effects of nearby water such as a stream, waterfall or fountain improves it even more.

WAYS TO ENJOY THE OUTDOORS

- ✓ Walking
- ✓ Gardening
- ✓ Bike ride
- ✓ Hiking
- ✓ Kayaking
- ✓ Sailing
- ✓ Golfing
- ✓ Kite flying
- ✓ Mining for gems
- ✓ Outdoor photography
- ✓ Metal detecting
- ✓ Team sports such as soccer

RESILIENCE RX™
Knitting Therapy

Knitting is a mindful activity that serves a number of therapeutic purposes. The simple act of focusing on the moment, repeating stitch after stitch, and turning yarn into something useful offers an escape for the mind with something to show for it.

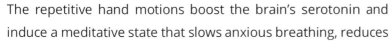

The repetitive hand motions boost the brain's serotonin and induce a meditative state that slows anxious breathing, reduces stress and depression. The bilateral, coordinated, precise movements of the hands and counting of stitches help preserve cognitive brain function and fine motor skills while the brainwork involved helps reduce ruminating thoughts associated with stress.

A survey of knitters and crocheters by the Craft Yarn Council found participants cited the following benefits from the hobby:

- ✓ 93% Feeling of accomplishment
- ✓ 85% Reduced stress
- ✓ 68% Improved Mood
- ✓ 56% Sense of confidence

BENEFITS

- ✓ Reduced depression and anxiety
- ✓ Increased sense of self esteem and well being
- ✓ Reduced loneliness and isolation
- ✓ Strengthened problem solving and decision making
- ✓ Promotes social connections
- ✓ Reduces cortisol, the stress hormone
- ✓ Slows anxious breathing
- ✓ Lowers blood pressure
- ✓ Distracts from chronic pain
- ✓ Provides sensory pleasure through soft, colorful yarn

NO JUDGMENT

The beauty of knitting is that there is no judgment. One can easily learn a simple stitch and immediately create a chain of stitches. Mistakes such as a mis-stich are easily fixed, and producing something tangible creates a sense of accomplishment and pride.

THE POWER OF PRAYER

One chilly morning in early 2006, Stacy Roorda, a busy 37-year-old mother of two little girls, noticed a strange lump in her left armpit. Having moved into a larger home some months before, Stacy attributed the pestering lump to nothing more than the strain of moving.

Nine months later, in November 2006, the odd lump hadn't resolved and Stacy's left arm felt achy. She finally gave in and made an appointment with her naturopath.

The doctor examined Stacy and was immediately suspicious of something sinister. She sent Stacy for a battery of urgent tests. The results rocked her world.

Stacy had breast cancer—stage 4, with metastases to the bone.

With two young girls at home, the oncologist planned immediate surgery to remove the cancerous mass in Stacy's breast.

Then the other shoe dropped.

Pre-op labs revealed Stacy was unexpectedly expecting—and the cancer was feeding on the very hormones her unborn baby needed to survive.

It was gloom and doom. Tears were shed, prayers were said, and she handed it over to God.

"I immediately got an image of a harness that racecar drivers wear," said Stacy. "The feeling was instant. 'Sit down and buckle up. It's going to be a rough road, but you'll be fine.' I grabbed onto that thought and never let go," she said.

Finding her case beyond his scope, the local oncologist sent Stacy and her husband south to Seattle.

Because the pregnancy hormone was the cancer's food source, the team of oncology specialists offered few options. Stacy's best chance for survival depended on immediate termination of the pregnancy followed by aggressive treatment.

They had no time to waste. The doctors told her it was her only hope. The cancer was too advanced.

It was either Stacy's life, or the baby's life. The doctors couldn't save both.

Against medical advice and to the horror of her loved ones, Stacy refused to abort the baby.

The doctors gave her three years to live at best.

News of Stacy's plight spread rapidly in her small hometown of Lynden, Washington.

With a 2-year-old and 4-year-old at home, and the very lives of Stacy and her unborn child at stake, family and friends sprang into action.

Meals were brought, childcare was juggled, and a church prayer chain was started.

Stacy was known for her devout faith. And her stubbornness. Despite pressure from the best oncologists in the state, she refused to terminate the unexpected pregnancy.

Having no choice, the team of oncologists ordered an older, less effective chemotherapy regimen that was deemed safer for the developing baby. Nicknamed Red Death, the goal was to slow down the cancer and buy Stacy time until the baby could be born. Treatment began immediately.

Back at home, news of the family's troubles spread. So did the prayer chain.

Though bolstered by the many petitions, Stacy wasn't about to be left out of the prayer party held on her behalf.

"Before every round of chemo, I would go into the bathroom by myself. I would take a few moments to look up directly to Jesus. You can always look around in the world and listen to the negative stuff, but if you look up to Jesus, that is where you find peace that surpasses all understanding. And I prayed that Jesus would fill the room with angels. I felt that as long as Jesus was there with me, I could do it," she said.

But after five rounds of Red Death, the baby started showing signs of distress. They had to stop.

Then, things went from bad to worse.

Already in her bones, an MRI showed that the cancer had advanced to Stacy's spine, and was marching downward. At just 32 weeks gestation, doctors needed to deliver the baby before the cancer reached the womb.

"Once again I was totally shocked. I thought back to the image of the seat belt. I had a very serious conversation with God," said Stacy.

"I don't remember signing up for this part. I've done everything you asked, and I've trusted you. You brought us through and we've been lifted up in prayer by loved ones and complete strangers around the world. How could this be?" she implored of God.

"Once again, I got the feeling God was indeed there and would bring me through it. He gave me a peace that surpassed all understanding, all I had to do was keep praying," she said.

By this time, reports of Stacy's dire situation had spread far and wide.

"I heard that my story reached missionaries, and that people around the world were praying. That was the most humbling part, knowing people were praying for me who had never met me. That's what carried Matt and I through the whole thing," she said.

With news that such a premature delivery was imminent, the prayers that surrounded Stacy and her family took on a new urgency.

Less than 48 hours later, Jazmine Stacy Roorda was born.

Weighing just 3.5 pounds and lacking the sucking reflex that hadn't yet developed, their tiny daughter was otherwise perfect.

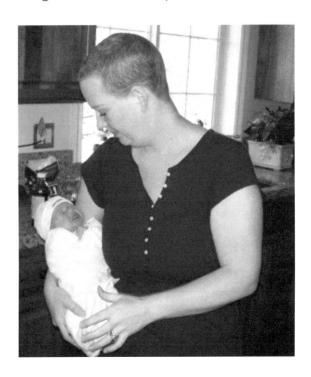

The announcement of the baby's birth spread along the prayer chain, but the petitions on their behalf didn't stop.

With the pregnancy behind her, two young daughters at home, a preemie in the NICU, Stacy now faced the cancer treatment head on.

The intensity of the prayer chain that now stretched around the world fortified Stacy's determination.

She believed without a doubt that the positive, loving energy contained in a prayer chain is a force that cannot be denied.

What happened next is what some might call a miracle: the treatment designed to buy Stacy a bit more time with her family instead brought the cancer to a standstill.

It hasn't budged since.

Fast forward sixteen years. Against the odds, Stacy not only survived the doctors' prognosis, so did her baby.

With bone mets, Stacy will never be free from cancer. But for reasons doctors can't explain, it fossilized in the various parts of her body.

Stacy gives much of the credit to the prayers that came from strangers across the globe.

What is prayer? It's love in an energetic form. Many use it to talk to God. Others use it to spread light in the world.

No matter how you use or label it, prayer is a powerful energy, love in its purest form.

"The power of prayer is how God works in this world, through people and their petition. Their desire to pray for a complete stranger is out of their love for Jesus. Love trumps everything," Stacy says.

Stacy Roorda is aware that skeptics are still waiting for proof in the power of prayer. But it doesn't faze her.

The prayer party that spanned the world on her behalf is all the proof she needs.

STACY ROORDA WITH DAUGHTERS HANNAH, ZOE AND JAZMINE (2019)

THE WAILING TENT

Dear grieving mother,

Welcome to the sisterhood of the wailing tent. With profound condolences, I know you'll soon forget my greeting, for your heart and soul have sustained a terrible blow.

The shock known as "the fog" will accompany you for some time, greatly impacting your memory. So I offer you this written welcome to refer to when your recollection falters.

The wailing tent is an honored place where only mothers with a broken spirit can enter. Admittance is gained not with an ID card bearing your name, but with the fresh sorrow etched on your heart.

Membership is free, for you have already paid the unfathomable price.

Directions to the wailing tent are secret, available only to mothers who speak our language of everlasting grief.

No rules are posted, no hours are noted. There is no hierarchy, no governing body.

Your membership has no expiration date, it is lifelong.

The refuge offered within its walls does not judge members based on age, religious belief, or social status. Hang your mask outside, and if you can't make it past the door, we will surround you with love right where you lay.

The wailing tent is a shelter where mothers shed anguished tears among her newfound sisters. A haven where all forms of wailing are honored, understood, and accepted.

In the beginning, you will be very afraid, and will hate the wailing tent and everything it stands for. You will flail, thrash about, and spew vile words in protest. You will fight to be free of the walls, wishing desperately to offer a plea bargain for a different tent, learn a different language. Those emotions will last for some time.

Your family and friends cannot accompany you here. The needs of the wailing tent are invisible to them. Though they'll try, they simply cannot comprehend the disembodied, guttural howls heard within.

In the beginning, your stays here will seem endless. Over time, the need for your visits will change and eventually you will observe some mothers talking, even smiling, rather than wailing. Those mothers have learned to balance profound anguish with moments of peace, though they still need to seek refuge among us from time to time.

Do not judge those mothers as callused or strong, for they have endured profound heartache to attain the peace they have found. Their visits here are greatly valued, for their hard-earned wisdom offers hope that we, too, will learn to balance the sadness in our hearts.

Lastly, you need not flash your ID card or introduce yourself each time you visit, for we know who you are. You are one of us, an honorary lifelong sister of the wailing tent.

Welcome, my wailing sister.

LYNDA CHELDELIN FELL (2014)

A01/THE WAILING TENT

JOURNALING PROMPTS

Use the questions contained in this section to record details you want to remember, or just to journal your thoughts, struggles, and triumphs. Keep your writing to yourself, or record every detail for safe-keeping, and compile and share it with family and friends when your heart is ready.

TIP:

- If a question is too triggering, consider skipping it for now and revisiting it at a later time when the question doesn't feel as raw.

- It can be helpful to answer the prompts from the perspective of what you want future generations of your family to know about your loved one and/or grief journey. If a future great-grand-child were reading this as an adult, what would you want them to know? Would your answers change if you knew that they, too, would experience loss of this caliber in their own lifetime?

- If you choose to journal for your eyes only, don't worry about using correct punctuation or being grammatically correct. Just pour your heart out for nobody else to read. If you wish to share it later, you can always rewrite your answers to clean it up.

- If you are struggling with what to write and can't write a paragraph, write a sentence. If you can't write a sentence, write a phrase. If you can't write a phrase, write one word that summarizes your feelings for the day.

MY LOSS

In order to fully understand our journey through loss, it is helpful to start at the pivotal moment that defines our before and after.

MY LOVED ONE'S NAME: _____

LOVED ONE'S BIRTH DATE: _____ DEATH DATE: _____

AGE AT TIME OF DEATH: _____ CAUSE OF DEATH: _____

MY LOVED ONE DIED ON _____

_____

WHERE I WAS AND WHAT I WAS DOING WHEN IT HAPPENED _____

_____

_____

_____

WHAT HAPPENED _____

_____

_____

_____

_____

_____

_____

_____

iCare

BIBLE JOURNALING

THE MEMORIAL

Planning our loved one's memorial presents emotionally-laden challenges shared by many. Choosing between cremation or a casket, picking a burial plot, holding a private unofficial remembrance or going with a full traditional funeral are but a few of the decisions we face. How do we get through the day, hour, minute? Use this chapter to record every detail.

THE DATE OF MY LOVED ONE'S MEMORIAL WAS

THIS DATE WAS CHOSEN BECAUSE

I CHOSE A CREMATION OR BURIAL BECAUSE

THE PEOPLE WHO HELPED PLAN THE MEMORIAL INCLUDED:

THE SERVICE WAS HELD AT:

THE SERVICE WAS PRESIDED OVER BY

THE PEOPLE WHO SPOKE AT THE SERVICE INCLUDED:

_____

_____

THE MUSIC WE SELECTED WAS:

_____

_____

THE POEMS, SCRIPTURES, READINGS WE SELECTED WERE:

_____

_____

THE MOST MEMORABLE PARTS OF THE SERVICE WERE:

_____

_____

_____

_____

_____

MY ADVICE TO FUTURE FAMILY MEMBERS WHO HAVE YET TO PLAN A LOVED ONE'S FUNERAL IS:

_____

_____

_____

_____

_____

_____

BIBLE JOURNALING

THE AFTERMATH

In the aftermath of loss, the intensity of our emotions and overwhelming sorrow threaten to engulf us and we wonder how we're going to survive. What do you remember from the first days, weeks and months after your loved one died? What emotions do you recall? How did you cope?

IN THE FIRST DAYS, WEEKS AND MONTHS AFTER MY LOVED ONE'S DEATH, I FELT

IN THE FIRST DAYS, WEEKS AND MONTHS AFTER MY LOVED ONE'S DEATH, I REMEMBER

IN THE FIRST DAYS, WEEKS AND MONTHS AFTER MY LOVED ONE'S DEATH, I COPED BY

MY FAMILY COPED BY:

WHAT I REMEMBER MOST FROM THIS TIME AND WHAT I WANT FUTURE GENERATIONS OF MY FAMILY TO KNOW:

_____

_____

_____

_____

_____

_____

_____

_____

_____

_____

_____

_____

_____

_____

_____

_____

_____

J04/SPIRITUAL JOURNALING

THE BELONGINGS

At some point many of us are faced with the task of sorting through our loved one's belongings. Whether we tend to this task immediately or put it off for years, every item large and small holds memories and we're faced with deciding what to keep, what to stow away, and what to donate or discard. When does the time come to address such an emotionally-laden task and how do we begin?

I SORTED THROUGH MY LOVED ONE'S BELONGINGS ON:

THESE PEOPLE HELPED ME:

MY LOVED ONE'S FAVORITE CLOTHING ITEM WAS:

MY LOVED ONE'S FAVORITE OUTFIT INCLUDED:

MY MOST CHERISHED ITEMS INCLUDED:

THE ITEMS I KEPT AS KEEPSAKES INCLUDED: _____

_____

_____

_____

_____

THE ITEMS I DONATED INCLUDED: _____

_____

_____

THE ITEMS I DISCARDED INCLUDED: _____

_____

_____

THE HARDEST PART ABOUT THIS TASK WAS: _____

_____

_____

_____

_____

_____

_____

_____

MY ADVICE TO FUTURE FAMILY MEMBERS WHO WILL FACE THIS SAME TASK IS: _____

_____

_____

BIBLE JOURNALING

THE TRANSITION

At some point following the loss of our loved one, we are faced with returning to a routine. Whether it be work, school, or caring for our family, transitioning from our old life to one without our loved one marks the period between what once was a familiar routine to new, unfamiliar territory.

AFTER MY LOVED ONE DIED, GETTING OUT OF BED WAS:

I TOOK THIS MANY DAYS OFF BEFORE RETURNING TO SCHOOL/WORK:

WHEN I RETURNED TO SCHOOL/WORK, THE EMOTIONS I FELT INCLUDED:

MY COLLEAGUES/ CLASSMATES/TEACHERS TREATED ME:

WHAT I WISHED THEY HAD KNOWN OR DONE DIFFERENTLY WAS:

THE PEOPLE WHO SUPPORTED ME/MY FAMILY THE MOST DURING THIS TRANSITION INCLUDED:

THE HARDEST PART ABOUT THIS TRANSITION PERIOD WAS:

MY ADVICE TO FUTURE FAMILY MEMBERS WHO WILL FACE THIS IS:

BIRTHDAYS & ANGELVERSARIES

Our loved one's birthday and death anniversary are predictably painful. No matter how long it's been, fresh waves of sorrow fill our hearts as if it happened yesterday. Some choose to spend the day in solitude, lost in memory about the moment his or her loved one left this world. Others choose to mark the dates with a remembrance activity such as a balloon release. How do we celebrate the life that lives on in our heart? How do we mark the date of our loved one's departure?

MY LOVED ONE'S BIRTHDAY IS:

MY LOVED ONE'S FAVORITE WAY TO CELEBRATE HIS/HER BIRTHDAY WAS:

MY LOVED ONE'S MOST MEMORABLE BIRTHDAY(S) WAS:

THE FIRST YEAR AFTER MY LOVED ONE DIED, I CHOSE TO HONOR HIS/HER BIRTHDAY THIS WAY:

NOW I MARK MY LOVED ONE'S BIRTHDAY THIS WAY:

THE PEOPLE WHO JOIN ME IN MY REMEMBRANCE ARE:

THE HARDEST PART ABOUT MY LOVED ONE'S BIRTHDAY IS: _____

_____

_____

_____

_____

MY LOVED ONE DIED ON: _____

THE FIRST YEAR AFTER MY LOVED ONE DIED, I CHOSE TO HONOR THE ANGELVERSARY THIS WAY: _____

_____

_____

_____

NOW I MARK MY LOVED ONE'S ANGELVERSARY THIS WAY: _____

_____

_____

THE PEOPLE WHO JOIN ME IN MY REMEMBRANCE ARE: _____

_____

_____

_____

THE HARDEST PART ABOUT MY LOVED ONE'S ANGELVERSARY IS: _____

_____

_____

_____

MY ADVICE TO FUTURE FAMILY MEMBERS WHO WILL FACE THIS IS: _____

_____

_____

_____

THE HOLIDAYS

The holidays come around like clockwork, yet treasured memories from years past can expectedly trigger a fresh wave of sorrow. If the grief is still fresh, holidays can be downright raw. How do we navigate the invitations, decorations, and festivities without our loved one?

MY LOVED ONE'S FAVORITE HOLIDAY(S) WAS:

MY LOVED ONE'S FAVORITE WAY TO CELEBRATE THIS HOLIDAY WAS:

MY MOST MEMORABLE HOLIDAY WITH MY LOVED ONE WAS:

THE FIRST YEAR AFTER MY LOVED ONE DIED, I CHOSE TO HONOR HIS/HER FAVORITE HOLIDAY THIS WAY:

NOW I MARK MY LOVED ONE'S FAVORITE HOLIDAY THIS WAY: _____

_____

_____

_____

THE PEOPLE WHO JOIN ME IN MY REMEMBRANCE ARE: _____

_____

THE HARDEST HOLIDAY FOR ME NOW IS: _____

_____

_____

_____

_____

_____

THE PEOPLE WHO HELP ME THE MOST THROUGH THIS HOLIDAY ARE: _____

_____

_____

MY ADVICE TO OTHERS EXPERIENCING THIS IS: _____

_____

_____

_____

_____

BIBLE JOURNALING

OUR FAMILY

In the aftermath of losing a loved one, our entire family is often impacted. Although bound by relations, we are all wired differently, and process loss in our own unique way. How was your family impacted by the loss of your loved one?

THE FAMILY RELATIONSHIP(S) THAT HAS BEEN IMPACTED THE MOST BY THIS LOSS IS:

THE FAMILY MEMBER(S) WHO STOOD BY ME THE MOST ARE:

THE FAMILY MEMBER(S) WHO STOOD BY ME THE LEAST ARE:

WHAT I WANT MY FAMILY TO KNOW ABOUT THE LOSS OF MY LOVED ONE IS:

MY ADVICE TO OTHERS EXPERIENCING THIS IS:

_____

_____

_____

_____

_____

_____

_____

_____

_____

_____

_____

_____

_____

_____

_____

_____

_____

_____

_____

_____

MY FRIENDS

In the aftermath of losing a loved one, friendships naturally shift. Some are strengthened as those friends offer a comforting shoulder and safehaven for our tears, while others fail us and fall away. How did your friends react to the loss of your loved one?

MY FRIENDSHIP(S) THAT HAS BEEN IMPACTED THE MOST IS:

THE FRIEND(S) WHO STOOD BY ME THE MOST ARE:

THE FRIEND(S) WHO STOOD BY ME THE LEAST ARE:

WHAT I WANT MY FRIENDS TO KNOW ABOUT THE LOSS OF MY LOVED ONE IS:

MY ADVICE TO OTHERS EXPERIENCING THIS IS:

BIBLE JOURNALING

THE DARKNESS

In the aftermath of losing a loved one, experiencing dark thoughts is common. While there would be no rainbow without the rain, how do we survive the storm?

AFTER MY LOVED ONE DIED, I EXPERIENCED THESE DARK THOUGHTS:

I TOLD MY DARK THOUGHTS TO:

THEIR REACTION TO MY DARK THOUGHTS WAS:

I SOUGHT HELP FOR MY DARK THOUGHTS THIS WAY:

I WORKED THROUGH THESE DARK THOUGHTS BY DOING THESE THINGS:

WHAT I WANT OTHERS TO KNOW ABOUT MY DARK THOUGHTS IS THIS:

MY ADVICE TO OTHERS EXPERIENCING DARKNESS AFTER LOSS IS:

BIBLE JOURNALING

MY FAITH

Grief has far-reaching effects in most areas of our life, including faith. For some, our faith can deepen. For others, it can be a source of disappointment. One commonality among the bereaved is that faith is often altered one way or the other. How has your faith been impacted?

I WAS RAISED WITH THIS FAITH:

SINCE MY LOVED ONE'S DEATH, MY FAITH HAS BEEN A SOURCE OF COMFORT OR DISAPPOINTMENT BECAUSE:

MY FAITH HAS SINCE CHANGED IN THIS WAY:

I WISH MY FAITH WOULD CHANGE THESE VIEWS ABOUT LOSS AND GRIEF:

THIS IS WHAT I WANT MY FAITH TO KNOW ABOUT LOSS AND GRIEF:

MY ADVICE TO OTHERS EXPERIENCING THIS IS:

BIBLE JOURNALING

MY HEALTH

As our anatomical and physiological systems work in tandem with our emotional well-being, when one part of our body is stressed, other parts become compromised. Has your grief affected your physical health?

PRIOR TO MY LOVED ONE'S DEATH, I CONSIDERED MY HEALTH TO BE

PRIOR TO MY LOVED ONE'S DEATH, I HAD THESE HEALTH ISSUES:

AFTER MY LOVED ONE'S DEATH, I DEVELOPED THESE HEALTH ISSUES:

SINCE MY LOVED ONE'S DEATH, THESE ARE THE STEPS I'VE TAKEN TO IMPROVE MY HEALTH:

WHAT I WANT MY DOCTOR TO KNOW ABOUT GRIEF IS:

WHAT I WANT OTHERS TO KNOW ABOUT GRIEF AND MY HEALTH IS:

MY ADVICE TO OTHERS EXPERIENCING THIS IS:

THE QUIET

Our loved one's absence remains day and night, but certain times of the day are harder than others. For some, it is evening or night when the house is quiet. For others, it is morning or afternoon. What time is hardest for you?

IN THE INITIAL AFTERMATH OF MY LOVED ONE'S DEATH, THE HARDEST TIME OF DAY FOR ME WAS:

NOW, I FIND THE HARDEST TIME OF DAY TO BE:

I FIND THIS TIME HARD BECAUSE:

MY ADVICE TO OTHERS EXPERIENCING THIS IS:

MY FEARS

In the aftermath of losing a loved one, fear can keep us focused on the past or worried about the future. If we can acknowledge our fear, we realize that right now we are okay. How do we control our fear so it doesn't control us?

IN THE INITIAL AFTERMATH OF MY LOVED ONE'S DEATH, MY BIGGEST FEAR BECAME:

NOW MY BIGGEST FEAR FOR MYSELF IS

MY BIGGEST FEAR FOR MY FAMILY IS:

I MANAGE MY FEARS BY DOING THESE THINGS:

THIS IS WHAT I WANT OTHERS TO KNOW ABOUT MY FEARS:

MY ADVICE TO OTHERS EXPERIENCING THIS IS:

iCare

BIBLE JOURNALING

MY COMFORT

In the aftermath of loss, what brings comfort one day can bring pain the next. Eventually we find a symbolic item or soothing ritual that offers a balm for the wound in our heart. What items or rituals bring you the most comfort?

WHEN MY LOVED ONE DIED, THESE ITEMS BROUGHT ME THE MOST COMFORT: _____

_____

_____

_____

THE ITEMS THAT NOW BRING ME COMFORT ARE: _____

_____

_____

_____

WHEN MY LOVED ONE DIED, THESE ACTIVITIES BROUGHT ME THE MOST COMFORT: _____

_____

_____

_____

THE ACTIVITIES THAT NOW BRING ME COMFORT ARE: _____

_____

_____

_____

WHEN MY LOVED ONE DIED, THESE RITUALS BROUGHT ME THE MOST COMFORT: _____

_____

_____

_____

THE RITUALS THAT NOW BRING ME COMFORT ARE: _____

_____

_____

_____

WHAT I WANT OTHERS TO KNOW ABOUT MY NEED FOR COMFORT IS: _____

_____

_____

_____

MY ADVICE TO OTHERS EXPERIENCING THIS IS: _____

_____

_____

_____

_____

_____

_____

J16/SPIRITUAL JOURNALING

MY SILVER LINING

In the earliest days following loss, the thought that anything good can come from our experience is beyond comprehension. Yet some say there are blessings in everything, every experience, including loss. Some experience a deeper relationship with their surviving loved ones that would never have happened if it weren't for the death of this loved one. Others develop a deeper faith, or a better understanding of humanity. Some find a stronger compassion for others. Have you discovered one or more silver linings in your loss?

DO YOU BELIEVE SILVER LININGS ARE POSSIBLE? IF SO, WHAT SILVER LININGS HAVE YOU DISCOVERED AS A RESULT OF YOUR LOVED ONE'S DEATH?

MY LOVED ONE'S DEATH HAD A POSITIVE IMPACT UPON THE LIVES OF OTHERS IN THIS WAY:

THE SILVER LINING I'M MOST GRATEFUL FOR IS:

MY ADVICE TO OTHERS ABOUT SILVER LININGS AFTER LOSS IS:

MY HOPE

In the aftermath of loss, hope can be hard to find. Yet every rainbow begins with rain, and every sunrise brings a ray of hope for a better tomorrow. Is hope possible in the aftermath of losing a loved one? If so, where do we find it?

BEFORE MY LOVED ONE'S DEATH, MY DEFINITION OF HOPE WAS: _____

_____

_____

_____

_____

NOW MY DEFINITION OF HOPE IS: _____

_____

_____

_____

_____

THESE ARE THE THINGS I NOW HOPE FOR MYSELF: _____

_____

_____

_____

_____

THESE ARE THE THINGS I NOW HOPE FOR MY FAMILY: _____

_____

_____

_____

_____

WHAT I WANT OTHERS TO KNOW ABOUT HOPE IS:

_____

_____

_____

_____

_____

MY ADVICE TO OTHERS ABOUT FINDING HOPE AFTER LOSS IS:

_____

_____

_____

_____

_____

_____

_____

_____

_____

_____

_____

_____

BIBLE JOURNALING

MY JOURNEY

The death of a loved one is a journey that's unique to each of us, and nearly impossible to describe to those who haven't yet weathered their own loss. What do you wish you had known about grief before losing your loved one? What do you want others to know about your journey through loss? How do you define your future?

WHAT I WISH I HAD KNOWN ABOUT GRIEF PRIOR TO LOSING MY LOVED ONE IS:

IF I COULD GIVE MYSELF ONE PIECE OF ADVICE ABOUT GRIEF, IT WOULD BE:

WHAT I WANT OTHERS TO KNOW ABOUT MY GRIEF JOURNEY IS:

MY ADVICE TO OTHERS JUST STARTING OUT ON THEIR OWN GRIEF JOURNEY IS: _____

_____

_____

_____

_____

_____

_____

_____

_____

_____

_____

_____

_____

_____

_____

_____

_____

_____

_____

_____

_____

_____

BIBLE JOURNALING

A LETTER TO MY LOVED ONE

Writing a letter to a deceased loved one can help you say and/or address things you didn't get a chance to and wish you had. Some find letter writing cathartic in that it allows the writer to express things or emotions they wouldn't say out loud, such as anger, guilt or shame. Others use letter writing as a way to connect with—or stay connected to—their loved one.

Use the prompts below to help you get started, or just write whatever is on your heart. Imagine your loved one sitting across the kitchen table. What do you want him/her to know? If you could go back and say something to your loved one prior to his/her death, what would you say? Write as many letters as you want.

PROMPTS:

- I am writing you to express my feelings regarding . . .
- I am writing to you to ask forgiveness for . . .
- I forgive you for . . .
- I want to thank you for . . .
- In closing, . . .

Dear _____

_____

_____

_____

_____

_____

_____

Love,

iCare

Dear _____,   DATE: _____

_____

_____

_____

_____

_____

_____

_____

_____

_____

_____

_____

_____

_____

_____

_____

_____

_____

_____

_____

_____

Love,

RESOURCES

LITERATURE & BOOKS

RESILIENCE RX™ – ONE SHEETS

Resilience Rx™ promotes evidence-based self-help techniques and positive coping strategies that support mourners through loss. Each one-sheet is a snapshot of the science behind the technique and how to implement it after loss.

Sold in packs of 10. Size 8.5x11"

1. Self Care Plan
2. Widows Self Care Plan
3. Coping with Isolation
4. Insomnia After Loss
5. Chromotherapy
6. Dance Therapy
7. Forest Therapy
8. Laugh Therapy
9. Sensorial Therapy
10. Hug Therapy
11. Music Therapy
12. Knitting Therapy
13. EMDR Therapy
14. Work Tips
15. Holiday Coping Tips

P07 | $15/10-PACK | InternationalGriefInstitute.com/resilience

ICARE COMMUNITY-BASED GRIEF SUPPORT GROUP

A community-based grief support group program for all loss types. Available at www.InternationalGriefInstitute.com.

MANUAL: $49.95

WORKBOOK: $19.95

iCare

GRIEF DIARIES AWARD-WINNING ANTHOLOGY SERIES

Grief Diaries is a ground-breaking anthology series featuring true stories about life losses and the many ways such losses impact our future. The diverse collection of stories raise awareness and shed critical insight into different types of losses while offering comfort and hope to readers who share the same path. Now home to more than 1000 writers in 11 countries, Grief Diaries and its sister series Real Life Diaries have earned seven literary awards and currently have 35 titles in print. See all available titles at www.icaremarket.com.

GRIEF DIARIES: SURVIVING LOSS OF A CHILD

Surviving Loss of a Child shares the poignant journeys of 22 women as they search for healing and hope after losing a child. Exploring how each mother faced a journey they couldn't fathom, **Surviving Loss of a Child** offers comfort and hope and is a reminder to others who find themselves facing the same journey that they can survive. Foreword by Grieving Men's R. Glenn Kelly.

$16.95 | ISBN: 978-1944328009 | icaremarket.com/product/100/

GRIEF DIARIES: THROUGH THE EYES OF A WIDOW

Through the Eyes of a Widow is a collection of tender stories by widows as they learned to adapt after losing her husband. Each shares the challenges, where she found the most help, and the hope she found along the way.

$16.95 | ISBN: 978-1944328641
icaremarket.com/product/101

GRIEF DIARIES: SURVIVING LOSS OF A SPOUSE

Surviving Loss of a Spouse features the poignant journeys of 15 men and women as they move through the aftermath of losing a husband or wife. Each narration offers a firsthand account of how each widow and widower faced the funeral, handled his or her spousal belongings, navigated the year of firsts, and how each fought to find hope in the aftermath. Foreword by award-winning playwright Carol Scibelli, author of *Poor Widow Me.*

MSRP $14.95 | ISBN: 978-1944328016
icaremarket.com/product/104

GRIEF DIARIES: SURVIVING LOSS OF A PARENT

Whether one loses a parent in the natural order of life or it occurs much earlier than expected, the emotional aftermath can challenge our fears, familial relations, and even our sense of self. **Surviving Loss of a Parent** offers 17 firsthand accounts that yield a powerful look at how such losses can influence every aspect of our life. Foreword by radio host and author Christine Duminiak.

$14.95 | ISBN: 978-1944328078
icaremarket.com/product/108

GRIEF DIARIES: SURVIVING LOSS OF A SIBLING

Losing a sibling is a heartbreak that leaves a hole in the fabric of every family. Facing a challenging journey that's often ignored cast into the shadows behind the bereaved parents, struggling through such emotions can be devastating lonely, **Surviving Loss of a Sibling** features the stories of 13 sisters and brothers as they fight to find the meaning of life without a sister or brother. Foreword by Benjamin Scott Allen.

$14.95 | ISBN: 978-1944328023
icaremarket.com/product/106

GRIEF DIARIES: THROUGH THE EYES OF MEN

Breaking the man code and offering readers an inside look into the hidden world of male grief, Through the Eyes of Men features the stories of 14 men of different ages who tackle the tender subject of male bereavement from the very moment their lives changed with a loved one's death. Foreword by Glen Lord, past president of the national board of directors of The Compassionate Friends.

$15.95 | ISBN: 978-1944328481
icaremarket.com/product/105

GRIEF DIARIES: SURVIVING LOSS BY SUICIDE

Three-time medalist, **Surviving Loss by Suicide** examines the aftermath of losing a loved one to suicide from the perspective of 12 different people. Voicing their thoughts and emotions through the funeral and beyond, each writer offers a candid look at a taboo journey. Foreword by award-winning author and suicide prevention advocate Emily Barnhardt.

$15.95 | ISBN: 978-1944328030
icaremarket.com/product/102

GRIEF DIARIES: SURVIVING LOSS BY OVERDOSE

Surviving Loss by Overdose is a compilation of stories by 12 people who answered 18 questions about losing a loved one to overdose in hopes of raising awareness, educating, and inviting society to offer survivors the compassion that's often denied in a stigmatized death. Forward by Elaine M. Faulkner, SUDP.

$16.95 | ISBN: 978-1950712076
icaremarket.com/product/103

GRIEF DIARIES: SURVIVING SUDDEN LOSS

Surviving Sudden Loss is a collection of 14 stories by parents, spouses, siblings, children, and grandparents who share their own personal insight into the hidden and often unspoken challenges of unexpectedly losing a loved one, including the emotional, mental, physical and social shifts they're forced to reckon with in the aftermath. With poignant narration, each writer shares the truth of their loss, where they found the most support, and how they rebuilt their lives in the aftermath. Coauthored by Maryann Mueller.

MSRP $18.95 ISBN: 978-1944328894
icaremarket.com/product/109

iCare

GRIEF DIARIES: SURVIVING LOSS BY CANCER

Surviving Loss by Cancer offers inspiring true stories about caring for a loved one with cancer all the way through to their final breath, and beyond. Filled with compassion and understanding, the collection of stories serves as a life raft in the storm of emotions, and offer readers hope, strength, courage after losing a loved one to cancer. Foreword by hospice director Dana Brothers.

$15.95 | ISBN: 978-1944328818
icaremarket.com/product/110

GRIEF DIARIES: SURVIVING LOSS BY IMPAIRED DRIVING

A silver medalist in the 2016 USA Best Book Awards, **Loss by Impaired Driving** examines the journeys of 17 men and women who lost one or more loved ones to a drunk, drugged or impaired driver. A must read for young, new drivers and for AA groups. Foreword by Candace Lightner, founder of MADD.

$15.95 | ISBN: 978-1944328269
icaremarket.com/product/112

GRIEF DIARIES: SURVIVING LOSS BY HOMICIDE

Surviving Loss by Homicide shares personal accounts of coping with a violent tragedy, and sheds insight into the strength needed to stay afloat in the aftermath of intense heartache and rollercoaster of emotions ranging from shock, anger, sadness and disbelief to healing and hope. Foreword by radio host Lady Justice.

$15.95 | ISBN: 978-1944328146
icaremarket.com/product/113

NATIONAL RESOURCES

ICARE MARKETPLACE
An online marketplace for memorial gifts and keepsakes.
www.icaremarket.com

GRIEF DIARIES
A vast collection of stories about surviving loss.
griefdiaries.com

WHEN YOU LOSE SOMEONE
A healing connection for all.
www.whenyoulosesomeone.com

ELLIES WAY
A nonprofit organization serving bereaved parents, grandparents and siblings.
www.elliesway.org

OUTSIDE WALLS
Resources and a ministry blog by Rev. Roland H. Johnson III.
www.outsidewalls.org

WIDOWLUTION
An organization dedicated to supporting widows.
widowlution.com

THE WIDOWERS SUPPORT NETWORK
An organization dedicated to helping widowers heal.
widowerssupportnetwork.com

OPEN TO HOPE
A nonprofit organization dedicated to helping people find hope after loss.
www.OpentoHope.com

NATIONAL ALLIANCE FOR GRIEVING CHILDREN
A nonprofit organization dedicated to serving bereaved children.
childrengrieve.org

TAPS
A nonprofit organization dedicated to helping families who lost a military member.
www.taps.org

SOARING SPIRITS INTERNATIONAL
An organization dedicated to supporting widows.
www.soaringspirits.org

UNKNOWN

We trust that beyond absence there is a presence.

That beyond the pain there can be healing.

That beyond the brokenness there can be wholeness.

That beyond the anger there may be peace.

That beyond the hurting there may be forgiveness.

That beyond the silence there may be the word.

That beyond the word there may be understanding.

That through understanding there is love.

PUBLISHED BY ALYBLUE MEDIA
www.AlyBlueMedia.com